SOULutions

A Supernatural Understanding for Conquering Chaos & Eradicating Self Sabotage

Michael R. Conner, M-RAS

Published by Miracon Enterprises
Los Angeles, CA
669-247-SOUL (7685)
miraconenterprises@gmail.com
www.miraconenterprises.com
www.michaelrconner.com

ISBN-10: 0982331622
ISBN-13: 978-0-9823316-2-0

Printed in the United States of America

The stories used in this book are real. The names have been changed due to confidentiality rules. In some cases, a story may represent a composite of one or more individuals.

Disclaimer: All information given in this book is strictly based upon the author's experience. Each individual and situation is unique in its own experience. The information presented here is not intended to take the place of a licensed professional. If there is ever a doubt about any piece of advice listed in this manuscript you are encouraged and advised to seek the help of a licensed professional in the field you are concerned about.

To my Dad,

For teaching me the importance of just "showing up."

To my friend; Robert Huff,

Because, you were that friend that "sticks closer than a brother."

Jodi,

Thank you For

being SOULution to

so many people!

To your

S.U.C.C.E.S.S.

Josh 1:8

CONTENTS

WHAT PEOPLE ARE SAYING
ABOUT SOULUTIONS

"Mike Conner is a pastor, Discipleship Program Director, as well as a certified drug and alcohol counselor with the State of California. He has a genuine heart for people and the Los Angeles Dream Center has been richly blessed with his passion for seeing people's lives healed and restored from life-controlling issues and addictions. His book is a powerful, yet practical book that shows the reader how to take the power of transformation through Jesus Christ and to be able to apply it to their lives.

—Pastor Matthew Barnett
New York Times Bestselling Author of; *The Cause Within You, Misfits Welcome* & *The Church That Never Sleeps,* Co-founder of The Dream Center in Los Angeles, CA & Senior Pastor of Angelus Temple

---

"It is with great pleasure that I recommend this book by Mike Conner to you. I can't say enough about how effective Mike has been in helping the hurting men and women at the Los Angeles Dream Center. He has a genuine love and compassion to see lives transformed from whatever life-controlling problem they may be dealing with.

This is an amazing book by someone who knows what he is talking about. In this book the reader will discover how to follow the same principles that have changed the lives of thousands of individuals who have come through the Dream Center Discipleship Program. In Mike's own words he states; *'Once you disciple someone to see themselves as God sees them, their life will never be the same again.'*

This book, is also a must read for any pastor, lay leader or concerned person that wants to help hurting people radically turn their lives around and walk in their God-given destiny."

—Pastor Tommy Barnett
Author of *The Power of a Half Hour, Hidden Power, Reaching Your Dreams, Multiplication,* & other books; Co-founder of The Dream Center in Los Angeles, CA; Sr. Pastor of Phoenix First Assembly of God in Phoenix; AZ, & Chancellor at Southeastern University in Lakeland, FL

Alcoholism and drug addiction place an enormous burden on everyone in our country. As the United States number one health problem, addiction strains the economy, the health care system, the criminal justice system, and threatens job security, public safety, marital and family life. Addiction crosses all societal boundaries, affects every ethnic group, both genders, and people in every tax bracket.

Alcohol is the most commonly used addictive substance in the U.S. 17.6 million people, or one in every 12 adults, suffer from alcohol abuse or dependence along with several million more who engage in risky drinking patterns that could lead to alcohol problems. More than half of all adults have a family history of alcoholism or problem drinking, and more than seven million children live in a household where at least one parent is dependent or has abused alcohol.

According to the National Survey on Drug Use and Health (NSDUH), an estimated 20 million Americans aged 12 or older used an illegal drug in the past 30 days. This estimate represents 8% percent of the population aged 12 years old or older. Additionally, the nonmedical use or abuse of prescription drugs--including painkillers, sedatives, and stimulants--is growing, with an estimated 48 million people ages 12 and older using prescription drugs for nonmedical reasons. This represents approximately 20 percent of the U.S. population.

Alcoholism and drug dependence can affect all aspects of a person's life. Long-term use of alcohol and other drugs, both licit and illegal, can cause serious health complications affecting virtually every organ in the body, including the brain. It can also damage emotional stability, finances, career, and impact family, friends and the entire community in which an alcoholic or drug abuser lives.

Mike Conner is one of the most prolific experts in the country when it comes to understanding the holistic approach to substance abuse and addiction. In this book Mike doesn't just talk about the problems, but gives practical solutions for the addicted. His down to earth approach has helped thousands of individuals find hope and freedom from their besetting behaviors.

I've known Mike Conner's for over forty years. His heart towards the hurting an afflicted has been consistent for all those years. This much needed information on how to help those in need is imperative for not only the addicted but for their families, neighbors and employers. This amazing information will help all those involved with someone living in the mire of such a debilitating lifestyle.

—Dr. Tom Jones
President and C.E.O. of City Rescue Mission in Oklahoma City, OK

Mike Conner is an amazing man who cares about hurting people and their recovery. Not only do I whole-heartily endorse his book but also count him as a good friend. I have seen how many people have been helped as a result of his compassion and experience. I have also had firsthand experience of seeing someone who was close to me have their life completely transformed as a result of going through the program this book is based upon. You cannot go wrong by getting this book. It will change your life or the life of someone you know that is struggling with life-controlling problems.

—Thomas Gehring,
Attorney & Author of *Settle It and Be Blessed* and *The Problem Solver*

"Once you see yourself as God sees you, your life will never be the same again!" Mike Conner has become a very dear friend of mine, one whom I deeply respect and he has played a very powerful role in my life personally bringing much breakthrough in a very delicate area of my life!

When Mike first spoke to me about his desire to write this book, I strongly encouraged him to not only write it but to publish it as soon as possible! Every human being wants to be a success, tragically too many give up because they are victims of what Mike calls "self-sabotage" or lose their way and become discouraged.

This book will give you practical, yet powerful supernatural applications from not only Mike's many years as a recovery pastor but also from an in depth study of the holy scriptures! It's time to reroute your life back into the pathways of success and beak the cycles of self-sabotage! Your new life awaits, grab this book and start reading it now!

—Jurgen Matthesius
Author of *PUSH: Pray Until Something Happens* and Senior Pastor of C3 Church in San Diego, CA

Mike Conner has been helping hurting people overcome life-controlling habits for over sixteen years. In his book, *SOULutions: A Supernatural Understanding for Conquering Chaos & Eradicating Self-Sabotage*, Mike shares the same, life-changing principles that have been used to help thousands successfully transform their lives. This book offers genuine *SOULutions* that will transform the chaos of addiction into freedom and hope. Mike's heart of compassion and years of wisdom shine throughout this easy-to-follow guide that will pave the road to healing and restoration.

—Danise Jurado
Author of *Fulfilled: Learning to Live the Life God Promised,* pastoral counselor & Transitions Program Director at The Dream Center in Los Angeles, CA

ACKNOWLEDGEMENTS

No undertaking of this magnitude can ever be acknowledged to the degree it deserves. For every one person that gets to stand in the spotlight with their fifteen minutes of fame, there are countless individuals who labor passionately behind the scenes. These are the persons making sure that everything goes according to the plans that have been set forth. With that in mind, I will begin my pathetic attempt to acknowledge the people in my life, who have helped shape my; attitudes, values, and beliefs in this book.

First I wish to thank God. Without Him guiding my steps this would have been an adventure in foolishness. It is my faith in Him that has given me the courage to face life and all the struggles that have lead to the successes in my life. I do not know, nor even care to imagine what my life could have been like if I had not turned it over to Him at such an early age.

Secondly, I would like to thank my wife Vilma, who has spent many tireless nights with me as we labored together on this project. Her love for me has been an anchor in times when I thought the storms of life would sweep me out to sea. I also want to recognize her encouragement in helping me to complete this book. I would also like to acknowledge her dedication to perfection. She has spent countless hours, not once, but many times, proof-reading the entire manuscript with her fearless red pen. I love you 'V'.

I also want to appreciate my daughter Michella, for sharing me with the hurting people I have had the privilege to help during most of her life. Her understanding and love for me has never wavered. Even when I was going through some of the most turbulent times of my life as a single parent, she would always have a word of encouragement for me. I am so thankful that you never bailed on me, even though you could have several times. I love you "Shella." I also want to publicly thank her husband, Ryan for taking up the leadership mantle in her life and for giving me two wonderful grandsons.

It goes without saying that my parents; Floyd and Rose, have played a significant part in shaping the person I have become. Without them creating a solid foundation in my life, this house would have crumbled a long time ago. I am also very grateful to them for their sacrifices and unconditional love, in spite of the much heartache I have put them through. Thank you Mom for all the sacrifices you made for me. Thank you Dad for your strength and belief in me, may you rest in peace, until we meet again.

In no way can I ever even begin to thank my former Pastor, friend, and lifetime mentor of forty plus years; Tom Jones. It is because of his contribution into my life that has allowed me to see and pursue the God-given purpose God created me for. He has the uncanny ability to see the greatness in people and literally pull it out of them. Thank you Tom for helping me get into alignment with my assignment and by believing in me even when I didn't believe in myself.

I also wish to thank my current Pastors; Tommy and Matthew Barnett. Without their encouragement to 'dream again' I would have never even dreamed of attempting something like this. They have given me the opportunity of a lifetime by allowing me to pour into the hurting men and women at the Los Angeles Dream Center. It is their belief in me that has allowed me to believe in others. Their legacy has impacted me in ways that I will never even know until I get to Heaven. Thank you Pastor Tommy and Pastor Matthew for taking a chance on me.

There are also many other people that I have had the privilege of knowing over my entire life that have poured into me. We are all products of the communities we have been a part of. For me to list all of them would be an effort in futility as there would be so many that would be left out. But I would like to acknowledge just a few more; Jed Nibbelink; thank you for taking a chance on me, Danny Ovando, thank you for your wisdom, Tom Gehring; thank you for your friendship, Steve Baker; thank you for your inspiration,

Michael & Lindsey Clifford; thanks for the use of your "Casita" during the writing process, Craig and Shelly Huey; likewise, I thank you for the use of "Chateau Huey" while writing this manuscript.

I truly am grateful to all of the people God has placed in my life over the years; past, present, and future. However, there is one special person I would also like to acknowledge. He was my best friend; Robert E. Huff. I really believe that as a direct result of his friendship, I am the man that I am today. It was this redneck from a burg in Ohio that taught me how to never give up on people. You are truly missed my friend and I can't wait until we see each other again in Heaven one day soon.

I would also like to thank the many men and women of City Rescue Mission and Dream Center Discipleship for giving me the privilege of pouring into their lives as they were struggling with alcohol, drug addictions, and other life-controlling issues. Some of you have been so patient as I learned along side of you what worked and didn't work. Throughout the many victories and disappointments I have learned that restoration is not just a process but a lifestyle. It will work if we can just learn to get past the layers of doubt that have us in bondage.

And lastly, I would like to thank you for choosing this book. I realize that there are many of these types of book on the market, and you could have chosen any one of them over this. I do not take that for granted and I appreciate the trust that you are showing me by choosing this book. What you have in your hand is more than a book. It has the potential to be a roadmap to success for you, if you will let it.

Just Do It! *Knowing if I don't do, He may not give me the same kind of opportunity again*

"I have been impressed with the urgency of doing. Knowing is not enough;
we must apply. Being willing is not enough; we must do."
—Leonardo Da Vinci[1]

A few years ago, I read where some undiscovered drawings of Leonardo da Vinci were found. It seems that some experts were examining one of his famous paintings[2] with infrared imaging. While doing this, they discovered there was another image underneath the painting. It seemed that he never stopped working. He would use whatever resources were at his disposal to get the job done, even if it meant recycling old paintings.

That is, what this book is about. Helping you start something and then using whatever means are available to help you see it through to the end. Being willing can only help provide the motivation to help get you started. You must choose to do something about your problems by taking initiative. This has been proven to be the best way on how to deal with difficult situations.

The life-damaging dilemmas you may be facing are not unique to you. It is not enough to just simply choose to start something. If you want real change, you must have a plan to succeed. And not just any plan will do. You need a SOULUTION that will help you accomplish that plan. You need a SOULUTION that will lead you out of bondage and into freedom. To do this, you must embrace the words of Aristotle; "*I count him braver who overcomes his desires than him who conquers his enemies, for the hardest victory is over self.*"[3]

I have been helping hurting people for more than sixteen years. During this time, I have had the privilege of serving those who are recovering from addictions and other life-controlling habits. As I look back over those years, I have seen a lot of miracles take place in my family, my ministry, and my life. I am so glad that God uses ordinary people, in unusual circumstances, to do extraordinary things. And, He does all this, so that lives can be miraculously transformed from the inside out.

This book is therefore a way of sharing some of those experiences with you. In it, I have tried to answer some of the more important questions I have had to address over the last few years. If you are struggling with addictions, or other life-controlling urges, there is hope for you. It is important to understand that these concepts, or SOULUTIONS, as I like to call them, do work. In fact, the reason they are being given to you in the form of this book is to offer you real and lasting freedom.

When I started working with people in recovery over sixteen years ago, I discovered something very disturbing. There are a lot more people who have problems in this area than we could ever even begin to imagine. Their faces are varied. The sucked-up junkie on skid row with a needle in his arm is not the only person needing help with this condition. Today, people come from all walks of life. From the crack addict in the gang-infested slums of South Central Los Angeles, to the polished preacher in Dallas, secretly addicted to pain medication. There is no bias in who is affected by this madness.

I have also come to realize something crucial that led to the creation of this book. There are a lot of people who don't have the money to spend on expensive rehab centers. And, if the twenty-eight day rehab programs are so successful, why aren't they working. Why are so many people going in and out of them, like revolving doors? It is common practice for someone to be in rehab for the second, third, fourth, and fifth time. There was even one person I worked with that had been in over twelve different rehabs.

You would think that overcoming addictions is a hopeless case. And if you believe in the disease concept of addiction, then your life truly is desperate. Because, according to that model, there is no cure. I, however, don't believe addictions are hopeless. I don't believe people who struggle with these harmful habits are hopeless or incurable. Mainstream addiction treatment programs will tell you that you have no hope. If you don't abide by the twelve steps and your treatment plans, you are doomed. You will repeat this vicious cycle over and over again.

While the twelve steps do work for some people, they are not the cure-all magic bullet. I believe that individuals must first come to a realization. And that realization is this. While you may be the one who has become addicted; the pain of your habit affects more than just yourself. You need to understand that you are now at the crossroads. The decisions you make from this point forward have the ability to change your life, as well as those close to you. Your choices can either catapult you into success...or destruction. The choice is yours.

As you read this book you are not going to be treated for your addictions. Rather, you will be educated on the thought process of finding supernatural SOULUTIONS for your problems and what that looks like to you. Some of these strategies will be controversial and definitely emotional. But in the end, they will prove to be lessons of love that will become a roadmap to your success. If you are still reading this book then chances are that I have peaked your interest. Either you, or someone you know needs help recovering from some life-challenging problem.

Reading this book will give you access to life-transforming SOULUTIONS. These are truths that will help you overcome these problems once-and-for-all. I know some of you might be wondering just what is so special about these SOULUTIONS. These are not just ideas or concepts, but they are profound truths that bring about change. And, just as that word implies, they reach into your very soul to deliver answers to the questions you have been too afraid to ask. These SOULUTIONS will help you identify the root issues you are dealing with. These issues are the reason for your pain that causes you to self-medicate.

I want to help you create a radical change in your thought process. This process will lead to a change in your behavior. I'm talking about a change that will lead you to *S.U.C.C.E.S.S.* This is an acronym I have come up with that means; **S**upernatural **U**nderstanding for **C**onquering **C**haos & **E**radicating **S**elf-**S**abotage. You need this kind of S.U.C.C.E.S.S. in your life in order to have your freedom back.

Supernatural Understanding

Since becoming an addictions counselor in 2007 I have learned a lot. I know a lot of the "best practices" out there only address the symptoms of addictions. But they fall short of discovering the actual reasoning behind those issues. And, it is those issues that we must deal with first. They are what fuel the destructive habits of addictions and other life-controlling problems.

The abuse of a substance, or anything else that causes dependency is just a symptom. It is an underlying cause of something much deeper going on inside of you. Whatever emotional trauma may be in a your life, it is a deeply-rooted spiritual problem. Letting God's supernatural power take you through the process of healing is the only thing that can solve this. Even addiction science itself, is beginning to change the way they treat people. They are beginning to see that trauma and environment have more to do with this than previously thought. Addictions are caused by more than mere genetics and mental disease.[4]

The first thing you will notice in this book is that you need to come to a Supernatural Understanding. You must shift your thinking by coming to this understanding. You must allow the Holy Spirit to take control of and transform your thoughts. I know that is not an easy task, but I am here to tell you it can be done. I have seen it with my own eyes. It is possible to renew your mind, and the Bible shows us how to do it.

Once you become aware of the transforming power of the Holy Spirit in your life, you are never the same. Your transformed thinking is now reshaping the way you process life. This leads you to rekindle the hope you once had. And to truly live in life, you must have hope. The apostle Paul spoke very clearly about hope in his writings. He even went so far as to say that hope is an anchor for our soul. To have success in this area you have to optimize the SOULUTION of H.O.P.E. You have to make it personal for yourself. This acronym stands for **Happiness**, **Optimism**, **Passion**, and **Excellence**. You must learn to hang on to each of these to cultivate this type of H.O.P.E. in your life. H.O.P.E. is necessary for you to have a supernatural understanding of God's plan for your life.

Once you have shifted your thinking and are hanging on to your H.O.P.E., you are ready for the next step. You must uncover your revelation. This revelation will help you to realize the buried potential of whom God created you to be. It is necessary to uncover this revelation to break free from the bondage and chains of addiction. They have kept you in captivity for way too long. In fact, without a revelation of who God created you to be, you are without boundaries and have no order in your life at all. You definitely need this supernatural revelation to start the transformation process.

Perhaps you are not sure that there is even a problem at this point. You are just curious to see what this book is all about. That is where having a supernatural understanding helps you. You cannot do this on your own. If you could, you would have done so a long time ago. It is time to come to an understanding that you need help from something bigger than you, a higher power, if you will.

I know some of you super-spiritual people are cringing right now that I used that word. If you have not figured it out by now, I am anything but traditional in my methods. Whether they are faith-based or mainstream, I know who my Higher Power is. It is up to you to decide to use a chair or a doorknob as your higher power. But, I have never known a chair or a doorknob to provide any help in developing a spiritual foundation. You need to establish a supernatural understanding or foundation in your soul first. Having done this, you can move on to the next area of your life.

Conquering Chaos

I'm not naïve enough to believe that these ideas are mine alone. They are a hybrid of theories, concepts, beliefs, and practices that have been developed over the years. This was accomplished through the process of elimination by seeing what works and what does not. It has definitely been a trial and error process. What you will read here may become a key that will help you take back control of your life.

But, let's just cut to the chase, shall we? The bottom line to all this is that you may not be convinced you are ready to change. You know that you eventually will. But now just doesn't seem like it's the right time. Besides, you're having way too much fun right now. And, you can hide, oops, I mean handle the negative things that go with this lifestyle. Can't you? Well, maybe you can and maybe you can't, but can you just humor me and continue reading for just a bit more? I think it will be worth your while. Besides, it's an easy read.

When you determine to conquer the chaos in your life, you are choosing to be in a continual learning mode. This is the only way that you will be able to see improvement in your life and the choices you make. This process will help you learn to love yourself. This is first accomplished by taking a good hard look in the mirror at who you really are. You must do this to influence your identity. You have to find out whom you are deep down inside. This practice is also good way to reveal your inner character. Your character is what drives your desires. You have to change your character to bring your desires into submission.

Then, once you find your cause, you are ready to unleash a revolution in your life. You are no longer living for just yourself. You have to unleash a desire from deep down in your soul that you are worth fighting for. You have worth, and you have a cause. You were created for greatness, so go and fight for it.

After you release your revolution, you must overcome the obstacles in your life. You do this by creating a lifestyle that will target you to a path of rebirth and renewal. This is necessary so

20

you can live for the future and not your past. However, you cannot start a revolution on your own. You need others to help you, and that is where this book comes in. You are also living to launch a legacy for others to follow. True transformation takes place when you are willing to step outside of yourself. You must make a pathway of success for others to follow. The best way to make this happen is to lead others in your success. Never get tired of your testimony. It is your story of success and it is what will help other people start their journey as well. ✂

Maybe you are already at that point in your life. You have found yourself struggling with an addiction and are ready for change. Ready for some hope of a sober, drug-free life. If that is you, then you can start today! Take action right now! Don't wait any longer! It is time for you to do something now to find your SOULUTION for life. Even if it's just working yourself up to discovering what your desire in life is.

You may be like a lot of people that cannot afford a traditional rehab treatment centers. And while there are hundreds of free ones, they usually require a commitment. Most likely, you will have a commitment of anywhere from six months to one year. But, you may have bills to pay and a family to support, so it is not affordable to make this type of a commitment. You are just not able to take the time off work necessary for that option to work for you.

Hopefully, this book can become a wake up call for your lost soul. Perhaps, even a roadmap to find your way back to wholeness. It can also become a SOULUTION to the question that you are desperately looking to find answers for. Or better yet, ways to help you find your way out of the confusion of chaos we call addictions.

This book is not so much about overcoming addictions and other life-controlling problems. Rather, it is about finding and dealing with the root causes of those destructive habits. As I stated before, these behaviors are just symptoms of something that goes much deeper. They are the end result of some pain that your tormented soul wants so urgently to numb. It is also about the process of restoration. It is about finding out who you really are so that you can be true to yourself and walk in your God-given purpose.

Eradicating Self-Sabotage

Whatever your reasons for reading this book may be, chances are, you have questions that need to be answered. Maybe these questions have come up before and you may have dismissed them to the back of your mind. I would even venture to guess that something happened recently that is making you consider that there might even be a problem here. Perhaps things were going great, life was good, everything was as it should be and then...something happened. This caused you to revert back to some old habits you thought were under control. But then again, this is not the first time this has happened to you, is it? In fact, I would guess that this has happened to you many times before. Hasn't it?

The ideas presented in this book, first became evident to me in my work at the City Rescue Mission in Oklahoma City, Oklahoma. I had first heard about this organization from a friend who preached at their chapel from time to time. I even accepted an invitation to go with him to one of the services he was preaching at. I am sorry to say that I only went one time and couldn't wait to leave. It was out of my comfort zone. In time, my friend became the President of that mission, and offered me a job to work there. I really don't know why I accepted the offer other than it seemed like an opportunity to make a difference in the lives' of people that were hurting.

At first I thought I had made a mistake because I had little in common that would have allowed me to relate to any of the people I found myself serving. Or so I thought. What I did discover was this; none of us really have it all together. We are all jacked up in some way or another. This became evident to me when I started out as the Education Director. I began to study the materials I would be teaching. As a result, some of the things I learned to help other people also helped me. They also applied to situations I found that were prevalent in my life as well.

I spent a total of four years working there. Those years were instrumental in helping to shape my foundation for recovery and restoration. The time I spent there created a different thought process within me. This led me to a much deeper level of understanding. I believe that to be the formation of the program we now have at The Dream Center. If you will do this plan, I have no doubt it will help you.

One of these principles I learned was very beneficial in helping me to succeed in my life. I needed to eradicate self-sabotage from every area of my thought process. This is an area that myself, as well as so many other people, can get caught up in. It is a dangerous web of deceit that happens way too often. If you want to be successful in every area of your life, then you have to defeat this. This is something that must be made a priority in your transformation process.

To be successful in this, you must learn to involve yourself in something bigger than you. This practice will cause you to connect yourself to a cause that is much greater than you. Let's face it. Addictions are selfish. You need to believe in something bigger than yourself. You need a greater cause. This is how you eradicate any hint of self-sabotage before it even begins.

After you have learned the importance of involving yourself in inconvenience, you are ready for the next step. You must learn to order yourself to make the right choices. Finding your SOULUTIONS for S.U.C.C.E.S.S. depends upon you being able to make right choices. But there is even something more important than making right choices. It is in making right choices, consistently. By doing this, you make a decision to choose your level of consistency. And, when you choose your level of consistency, you can and will, change your desires. You can go from practicing bad habits, to good ones.

And finally, you have to be brutally honest with yourself by neutralizing all negativity in your life. You do this by identifying and eliminating all the excuses in your life. You can't let anything derail your focus. You have to stand against the very gates of H.E.L.L. You must eliminate your Hate. After that, you need to eliminate any sense of Entitlement you feel you have. It will not serve you well. Pride is what keeps addictions in chains. You must humble yourself in order to do this.

Next, you will need to eliminate all Lack from your life. I'm not talking about a prosperity gospel message here. I'm talking about living in an atmosphere of gloom, defeat, and agony on me attitude. Now here's the really tough one. You must eliminate your Lust. Lust, at its <u>base form is just a strong desire to do things your</u> <u>shouldn't do</u>. That has to be erased from your thought life. <u>That will cause you to self-sabotage quicker than anything.</u>

Conclusion

There is one final area I want to make sure you understand. That is the concept of grace. Grace is so important because without grace, change is not possible. But, in situations such as this you need something more. You must learn to accept the **audacity** of grace. You are not a failure and you should not go around feeling like you don't deserve success. Jesus gave the ultimate sacrifice so that you could achieve success and have right standing with God again.

Grace is a gift. It is not something you have to earn. It is God's unmerited favor, but it even goes beyond that. It is the desire and ability to do God's will. And His will is quite simple, to know God, and to make Him known to others. What you really need in order to accomplish this is alternative SOULUTIONS to mainstream recovery. Knowing what these SOULUTIONS are can help you right now, with whatever you may be dealing with.

In these pages, I have put years of experience to work in developing an easy-to-follow guide that will lead to your restoration. I have taken the best strategies or what I call SOULUTIONS, of a yearlong program and condensed it into a book that has the ability to help you get your life back on track. These are the same practices that have helped thousands of individuals find help for their renewal and healing. I must warn you, this is not a quick fix, but the beginning of a new lifestyle. These SOULUTIONS have been used not only at the Dream Center, but also in other organizations that have produced a documented 80% plus success rate. You should know that those kinds of numbers are very rare in this field.

So, if you're ready to receive your SOULUTION, then let's continue to the next section. It just might have some answers you've been looking for. Oh, and don't forget to M.A.P. your SOULUTIONS at the end of each chapter. This is where you take a moment to reflect what you have just read and M.A.P. it out. It will help put things in perspective as to where you are and where you need to be. M.A.P. stands for; **M**ake a plan, **A**ccountability partners to help you with your plan, and then **P**ut your plan into action. To your S.U.C.C.E.S.S.!

Supernatural
Understanding
Conquering
Chaos
Eradicating
all
Sabotage

Happiness
Optimism
Passion
Excellence

- God's supernatural healing (take you through the process of healing (trauma + environment)

Hate
Entitlement
Lack
Lust

Footnotes

[1] *Getting Motivated to Change,* (Fort Worth, TX, TCU Institute of Behavioral Research, 2006), page 2.

[2] http://news.bbc.co.uk/2/hi/uk_news/4639945.stm, accessed 9/5/2015

[3] *Getting Motivated to Change,* (Fort Worth, TX, TCU Institute of Behavioral Research, 2006), page 3.

[4] HuffingtonPost.com. (2015, January 20). Hari, Johann. ***The Likely Cause of Addiction Has Been Discovered, and It Is Not What You Think.*** Retrieved on 9/5/2015 from http://www.huffingtonpost.com/johann-hari/the-real-cause-of-addicti_b_6506936.html.

A SUPERNATURAL

UNDERSTANDING

*"By wisdom a house is built, and by
<u>understanding</u> it is established;
and by knowledge the rooms are filled
with all precious and pleasant riches."*
Proverbs 24:3-4

"Any fool can know. The point is to <u>understand</u>."
Albert Einstein

CHAPTER 1

SHIFT

Transform Your Thinking

*"He is no fool who gives up what he cannot keep
to gain that which he cannot lose."*[1]
— Jim Elliott, Missionary

Oscar grew up in a family that provided his basic necessities and made sure that he was well taken care of. His Parents had divorced when he was a young child and his mom remarried his stepfather a few years later. Oscar played sports and did a lot of activities as a kid.

Somewhere along the way, his friends that played sports or just hung out with him with started to change. They began experimenting with drugs and some of them were "jumped" into gangs. Even thought his mom was busy working, she found the time to give him the "do's and don'ts" as he would later call them. But Oscar felt she never showed him not the "how to's" in life.

Oscar learned these on the streets. He learned how to use drugs and how to get involved with gangs. He also learned how to lie, how to cheat, how to steal and everything else in between. He knew he needed to change, but never had the desire and things just kept getting worse. During this time Oscar was arrested many times. He started going into drug rehab programs. Then one day, something special happened.

Oscar saw this guy that he knew from school preaching the gospel everywhere on the streets. So one Sunday, he decided to go to church with this man. He used to be a gang member and Oscar had seen the change in his life take place from a distance. He was a Christian and Oscar was watching him and saw that it was genuine. Then one day, at twenty-one years of age, Oscar finally invited Jesus into his heart to be the Lord of his life.

Things began to change, but not as you may think. It seemed as if he had entered into a war. He wasn't doing very good and was struggling at serving God. Later, through a series of circumstances, he ended up in prison. After serving his time, he got out and started to going to church again. But soon, he was back in prison again. This cycle continued to be a constant in his life. It almost felt as if we was going through a revolving door.

It was during this time of going in and out of prison and church, he found out about our program. Oscar had been in "programs" before, but this one seemed different. So he stored that message in the back of his mind. After all, this is something he would need to know about to send other people that needed it worse than him.

After spending nine months in a program and then leaving it in 2008, Oscar went back to his home church. The one where the gang member he had met so long ago was now the Senior Pastor. He thought he had it all together and everything was going well. He even fell in love and got married to his beautiful wife. He continued to be clean and sober and soon had a child on the way. He was being discipled by one of the mightiest men of God on the planet he knew. Life was good.

As he settled in and grew comfortable, he began to let down his guard. The enemy then used that to start creeping back into his life again. He began to doubt God's word. That doubt turned into arguments, and those arguments turned into leaving the church. After leaving the church, Oscar relapsed and found himself in the bondage of drugs once again. That relapse soon sent him down a dark path. Things got so bad, he soon had a restraining order from his now, pregnant wife. Things continued to spiral downward and Oscar violated his restraining order. This ultimately turned into a jail sentence.

He found himself lying on the floor of a jail cell. He was shattered and crushed on the inside. He felt overwhelmed by the feelings of brokenness and sadness. He decided that he was defeated and it was time to throw in the towel. But instead, something utterly amazing happened. Jesus picked it up and threw it right back to him! Time passed and his mind began to heal from a very long drug binge. He decided that it wasn't time to quit just yet.

When he got out of jail and came to us for help. He needed the discipline and structure that we were able to provide. The best part about being here was that the discipline was mixed with so much love. Oscar felt like he was part of a huge special family. He learned so much more from being here than he could have ever imagined possible. He developed life-long friendships with men he met here that he considered to be his brothers. Each and every one of them had an impact upon his life.

The leaders taught him how to walk in love and serve others. He learned to not be so rigid and militant with his Christianity. The leaders also demonstrated wise leadership by applying firm but necessary correction. All this was done with so much love and compassion. Every person there was used by God to change his life!

Before he knew it, the year was over and Oscar had finished his time here. He went back home to be with his family and serve his local church. As I am writing this, Oscar has been back home for a few years now. It hasn't been easy, but the discipline he learned while he was with us, has been the backbone of his success. It has also been foundational in helping him to apply the principles of the Bible in his everyday life.

Oscar is now worshipping God with his family at church (without a restraining order). He gets to see his kids on a regular basis. He is still clean and sober. He has his own car and rents a nice place about a mile from the church he attends. He is now off of probation and has completed all the requirements of the probation department. God has also opened up a door for Oscar to work part time and go to college full time. He loves every minute of what God is doing in his life these days!

Transform Your Belief System

Oscar realized that to succeed, he needed to reshape his mind by transforming the way he thought. This is a universal truth that applies to everyone, regardless of your struggles. Oscar took to heart the quote at the beginning of this chapter. He understood that God had given him something that could never be taken away.

I recognize there may be some of you reading this that may have never heard of Jim Elliott or his wife Elizabeth. The quote I just referred to at the beginning of this chapter is from Elizabeth Elliot's book. It is about a man who was willing to risk everything in order to follow what he believed was God's will. He willingly did this even though it cost him his own life. This was not just a saying by someone who thought of something clever to say in a book. To Jim Elliott, it was a way of living for him. It was a principle that he lived and died by. He chose to even gamble his own life in order to help others know God and the power that delivers them.

The Elliot's were sent to be missionaries to South America. Not just any tribe, but a savage one that had never heard the Gospel of Jesus Christ. What made this, such an urgent mission, was the fact that the tribe was in danger of wiping themselves out. They believed in settling their arguments with the end of a spear. It was not unusual to kill a whole family over a single misunderstanding.

One day, as they were making contact with the Indians, they were attacked. Jim and his whole party were killed. This happened in spite of the fact they had guns to protect themselves. They had already discussed among themselves what to do if they were attacked. They would rather give up their lives and gain heaven than kill someone. They did not want to be responsible for sending one single Native to hell by their defensive actions.

Their belief system was based on something more than most people can understand. Or, for that matter, even read in a book. But I may be getting ahead of myself here. Let me explain exactly what a belief system is. The best definition I found comes from a book called; *Advanced Life Skills*. It defines it this way; "...a structured process by which we evaluate everything in our lives. We develop our own system of beliefs based on how we interpret the world around us according to our observations and experiences[2]."

I'm going to make another bold statement here. Are you ready? Our belief systems have nothing to do with the Bible whatsoever. Let me clarify this statement for you. Part of that belief system may have been influenced by your past. Such things as may have influenced you are; reading the Bible, going to church, or by being raised in a Christian home. But in the end, we are the ones that decide what we are going to believe. Like the quote says, we develop these belief systems because of what we have experienced and seen. The reason it is important to understand this, is that we tend to develop wrong belief systems.

A belief system is something you get deep into your soul. It is something you have determined to believe in that works for you. Don't get me wrong. I am not saying that faith is not involved here. But you can have faith in anything besides the Bible and God. You have to allow what you believe, become so real to you, that you can't even consider another option. You believe it; therefore, it is real to you.

That statement is also another reason why someone else's SOULUTION, may not work for you. Your belief system could initially be from someone else, but in order for it to work for you, you must own it. You must let it become part of who you are. It must fit in with what you have seen and what you have experienced. It becomes part of who you are as a person. You will have a hard time separating your belief system from yourself. It is part of you.

In the early days of your life, you may have believed what you were told by your family or taught in Sunday school. But you had not made it part of your personal belief system yet. You had never experienced a particular truth firsthand for yourself. As a result of this, you may have decided to do away with some of those beliefs altogether.

They weren't working for you, and you needed something that would. That led you to develop your own system, based on what you believed was working for you at the time. For most of you, it may have been whatever method was helping you cope with stress or some pain in your life. If you are like most people I deal with, that usually took the form of some chemical or substance. You needed this to help you cope with whatever you were going through.

To transform your thinking, you have to forget some of those things. They may have worked in the beginning. In fact, they still may be working for you. But if you are reading this book, then I think you have come to the belief that the price is too high to keep using it. And if it didn't work for you, then it became part of the problem that was helping to fuel your addictions. To change what you are doing, you have to rewire the pathways in your brain.

The way that science teaches us to do this is to find a new behavior and turn it into a habit. You do this by repeating it over and over and over again until it becomes an automatic response. It is kind of like the way that prospective soldiers are trained in boot camp. Your training must include choosing a new belief system to live by that will help you get to where you want to be. You need a new behavior that works for you and your situation. But is must be based upon truth, instead of your feelings. Truth will not change, but your feelings can change minute by minute.

The best way I found to do this is by looking to the Bible. The Bible is full of individuals who struggled with life like we do. They were misfits, outcasts and drunks who God called to make a difference. In spite of whatever crises they were going through at the moment, God used them.

Just look at this list. Noah got drunk. Abraham was old. Sarah was impatient. Jacob was a cheater. Moses was a stutterer. Miriam, his sister was a gossiper. Samson was a womanizer. Gideon was insecure. Jonah ran from God. Elijah was bi-polar. David was an adulterer and a murderer. Peter had a temper. Thomas was a

34

doubter. Saul (Paul) was a religious psychopath. Lazarus was dead, that was probably the only legitimate reason in the whole bunch. These men grew up knowing about God, and in some cases, even having a relationship with Him at one time.[3]

But something happened to them that shook their belief system. They needed to find something to believe in. Something, that maybe they had either forgotten, or never experienced in their life yet. They did not come to experience a new belief system for their situation, until they had a crisis of belief. Then, they transformed their negative circumstance into a positive one. They did this by owning a belief system that basically said; with God, they could do anything. But to them, it was more than a belief system. It was who they were, or had become through the process of transforming their thinking.

Let me give you an example of this. I love acronyms. I really cannot tell you why. They just make sense to me. To me, it is a way to teach people to remember things. If you look at the first letter of each chapter title, it is an acronym for the title of this book. It spells out; S-O-U-L-U-T-I-O-N-S. That is what this book is about. I use them as a tool to help people remember the points I am making. A little further down in this chapter I am going to share another one with you. Maybe, it will help you remember something about this chapter and life in general.

But my point is this, people that know me, are aware that using acronyms is part of my belief system. It is something that works for me and helps me explain what I believe in. In fact, as I am writing this section, I noticed something just now. A graduate of our program posted on Facebook and tagged me about this very subject. I get teased all the time about it. But at the end of the day, it is who I am. I love it and own it at the same time.

When people that have been through the program hear an acronym. I can almost guarantee you; they will smile and think of some lesson I taught using one. Not so much because I am a great person or a terrific teacher. They will do this because one of those acronyms helped them learn some truth during the time they were here. That is why I do this. It is about knowing God and making Him and His truths known. That is how I want to be remembered.

Maybe you were that individual learning to live in the moment. You were willing to take a chance with your life. You did this just to satisfy some craving that let you escape from reality for a few hours. And the truth is, living in this reality scares you more than the possibility of losing your life. Life is too hard and what you have been doing has not been working out too well for you. Be truthful with yourself here. What is your truth? What is your belief system? Will it help you or kill you? Or does it just hide the pain for a little while?

Or, perhaps, you are the loved one or a close friend of someone who fits the description I just talked about. Regardless of who you may be, there is a SOULUTION for you. This book has been written to share some radical ideas that will transform your thinking.

My hope is that these ideas might just give you the answers you have been looking for. Answers that, if used the right way, can be a drastic new beginning for what God has in store for you. I challenge you to trust God with your beliefs. He knows whom He is and is not worried about what you believe about Him. He loves you and wants to see your life transformed.

Transform Your Trust

Trusting God is *never* an easy process. It involves an element of risk on our part that we most likely are not willing to take. We do this even though we know the rewards are generally worth the risk. We will choose to stay in our mess because it is something we are familiar with. It is something that requires less of us. The path to freedom and transformation is a difficult path that few are eager to walk.

"How much are you willing to trust in order to gain your freedom? Specifically, I'm talking about freedom from life-controlling issues that are keeping you in bondage?" That was the question I presented to someone I will call "Keith." We were in the middle of one of the many session I have had with individuals in our program. They, like you, are struggling to get free from the destructive stronghold of addiction.

"What do you mean?" was his answer. I said, "Keith, in my dealings with people who struggle with addictions, there is one thing in common. There is almost always an element of risk involved. Whether it's the police who are trying to catch and send you to jail. Or, it may be public humiliation; such as having your arrest televised on the six o'clock news.

"Then there is also the other side of the coin that we don't like to think about. Someone we trust, such as a pastor, being caught in a compromising situation. They both have one thing in common. They are willing to risk everything for that brief moment of pleasure. It may be just an escape from the mundane reality we call life.

"But yet, these same people have trouble when it comes to trusting. They won't trust God, family members, or friends who are trying to help them. They would rather believe somebody on a street corner delivering death. Or better yet, a bartender in a place where 'nobody knows your name,' or even cares to know it, for that matter. All they care about is that you pay the bar tab and leave them a nice tip. They prefer to trust people like that instead of people that love them in spite of what they've done. And, these are people, who may have known them for most, if not all their life. Why is that Keith?"

I paused to give him some time to reflect on what I had just said and to give him time to come up with an answer. "I'm not sure I know the answer to that." was his reply. So I pushed the point a little farther. "Why do *you* do that?" I asked. "Wow! You really don't pull any punches, do you?" Keith questioned. But I could tell he was dodging the answer, so I continued to push. "Let me help you answer that. We are strange creatures with no rhyme or reason for what we do. We tend to do what we do regardless of the consequences. We do it because it seems like the thing to do at the time.

"We will even encourage other individuals to join in our quest to spin the roulette wheel one more time. We will do this, for no other reason, than the expectation of euphoria for one more brief moment in time. In other words, we are willing to risk it all for something uncertain. We would rather do that than trust in something that is tried and true. But, that's not nearly as exciting as living on the edge, is it?"

I could tell I had his undivided attention, so I continued. "Believing in others, or even in themselves is something that is a foreign concept to them. But that's OK, there are a lot of people who struggle with trust issues. Is that statement true in your case?" I asked him. His reply surprised me and caught me off guard at the same time. "No, I trust people." he said. "I just don't trust myself." "Why not?" I asked him. "It's not that easy to answer." came back his reply. Try as I might I couldn't get him to elaborate on his response.

I finally decided to speak. "Keith, I have found in my experiences with helping hurting people, that abuse from an early age may causes this. They blame themselves and this will sometimes prevent them from forgiving and believing in themselves. This also carries over into their relationships with other people. It will even mutate into the spiritual realm by causing them not to believe in God. It is rare to find someone coming out of abuse and addictions to have blind faith in their caregivers. This usually will only happen when a person has exhausted all other means of finding help, and are on their last leg of hope.

"We have trouble seeing ourselves as God sees us. I think that is why we don't pursue Him wholeheartedly. If we understood the plans and purposes that God has for us, we wouldn't give up. We would be lining up for miles to get a glimpse of the future He has prepared for us. Instead, we prefer to wait in line, for the latest video game machine. Something that will only further tune us out from the reality of pain, we are trying to hide.

"Keith, I feel so strongly about the concept of risk that I am going to risk something myself. Instead of telling you a story about someone else I am going to take a risk and trust you. I'm going to do this by telling you a little bit of my story. Being transparent is generally not something people find as an easy task. However, I will do my best to share part of my story, even though it is, still at times painful for me. But I like you and want to help you. So here goes."

Transform Your Outlook on Life

Life is not always a journey of joy. In fact, it is often a street scarred with the potholes of compromise and complacency. My story is not much different in the beginning than a lot of the people I help on a daily basis. I was raised in a good Christian home, in a very strict Pentecostal church. My family had been in the same denomination for three generations. This started from my grandparents on both sides, down to myself. I was also a third generation preacher in this same organization. An organization, which was at times, was known for its exclusivity and harshness. Although, I am grateful for the godly heritage that was passed down to me, this was an environment that unintentionally set me up for a failure.

I had felt the calling into ministry at the young age of sixteen. So, I decided to go to our denomination's Bible College after graduating High School. Upon completion of my studies in college I found myself ministering in Louisiana. It was here where I met the woman who would become my wife and the mother of my child. We were married after a whirlwind romance. Which, at the conclusion of, resulted with her becoming a preacher's wife.

She was not raised in our organization, so she had no hint of what she was getting herself into. I didn't help matters any because in those days you were supposed to take care of ministry first. And, if you did a good enough job, God would reward you by helping to take care of your family. It came as no surprise that our marriage ended. What was surprising to me as I look back on it was the reality that it lasted for nine years.

I was shattered beyond belief. The fact that you see something coming does not weaken the impact it has when it finally crashes into you. How could I have been so naïve as to trust my dreams and future with another human being? I was now an outcast — a minister who could not keep his family together. Thus I was no longer of any use to the denomination I had grown up in and known my entire life.

After a feeble attempt at trying to heal within that organization, I eventually left. I was a wounded warrior trying to make sense of being spiritually shot. As a result, I was left emotionally handicapped for the rest of my life. I know that may seem harsh, but that is how I felt. The teachings of that denomination prevented me from having any hope for my future. I wasn't allowed to remarry unless I reconciled to my first wife. To me, it was more than a set of rules or teachings. It was my way of life. The only way I had known to that point.

Also, at that time in my life, transparency was a foreign concept to me. I wasn't familiar with it because, you didn't discuss your personal and private life with others. This was especially true if you were in a ministerial position. Not being able to share with my peers what I was going through made me feel as if God Himself had forsaken me. Feelings of rejection, low self-esteem, and humiliation were my constant companions. I didn't know which way to go because my world had been turned upside down.

I no longer knew what was right, wrong, or even acceptable at that point in my life. It seemed as if there were more don'ts than do's at the church where I was going. It truly was a spiritual bondage. So I decided to take a risk and search for a new church home.

What does it mean to risk? The dictionary defines the verb risk as: *to expose the chance of injury or loss; to venture upon; take or run the chance of[4].* The concept of risk has been around for quite a while. Since the beginning of time, men have struggled with what it means to truly risk it all. Adam took a chance to trust Eve that it was okay to take the first bite of that forbidden fruit. Samson took a risk to tell Delilah the secret of his strength. Ever since the beginning of time, mankind has been learning to live with the question, *"Is it worth the risk?"*

For some, risk may mean getting enough courage to ask someone out on a date. For others, the meaning might be as simple as crossing the street without looking both ways. And then there are the radical risk takers. You know the type. These are the adventurous individuals who look fear straight in the eye and just do it.

They are prepared to take the risk no matter what the cost may be. They are willing to go skydiving, base-jumping or bungee jumping. They are willing to risk their safety for a brief encounter of excitement. They are after the thrill and feel that the adrenaline rush will give them for that one moment.

There are also those who have moved beyond the adrenaline rush. They have moved into something a little more chemical. This goes beyond the everyday routine and borders on insanity. These are the individuals that are pushing the edge. They ponder with increasing the amount of substance they are about to consume. They are willing to do this because that last hit didn't quite take the edge off of the pain they were feeling. The same pain they are trying hard to forget.

Why is risk such an important part of understanding how to transform your thinking? If you had asked what risk was prior to this time in my life, I would've told you something different. For me, it was a board game I used to play in college with my roommates. What I was going through now was so surreal.

How do you pour out your heart and soul to a perfect stranger that you just met? Especially, at the back door of the church as you are leaving? Needless to say it took awhile before I opened up to anyone. "I was too vulnerable. I needed time to heal. I'll make an appointment next week." Those were actually some of the excuses I used to avoid talking to people. And, I would never get involved at the various churches I attended.

Ultimately a coworker noticed what I was going through and invited me to her church. I finally ran out of excuses and gave in. I initially only went just to check out their Christmas production. I was blown away and captivated by the compassion everyone there showed me. They made me feel like I was the most important person to them. I later learned they were modeling their church after another church in Phoenix, Arizona.

As a result of their love and compassion, it wasn't long before I was attending there on a regular basis. I was introduced to the pastor and before I knew it, had set up an appointment to meet with him and share my deepest, darkest secrets.

Transform Your Concept of R.I.S.K.

The time had come for me to trust again. It was time to learn how to trust again, to take a R.I.S.K. — 1) Reveal who I was to a total stranger, 2) Involve myself with something bigger than myself, 3) Serve others without respect to who they are or what they could do for me, and 4) Kill all negative self talk – against myself and others.

Revealing who you are to another person is more difficult than it seems. There is definitely an element of risk in that. In my mind I had nothing to lose. I didn't know this man and he didn't know me. I had only been to the church a few times. So if things didn't go as I had planned, then I could walk away with no emotional involvement. So, it was with that in mind that I determined to bare my soul to a man who would soon become my new friend and pastor.

It wasn't easy as I shared about my upbringing and most recent tragedies that had left my soul wounded and emotionally exposed. Before I knew it I was revealing my fears and dreams and hopelessness all at the same time. He must have thought that I was a spiritual schizophrenic. As we concluded our session, he leaned forward and said something I did not expect to hear. "You are called to do ministry, and you will never be happy until you are doing ministry again." He then went on to say something else. "This church is a church with a heart and a church of action. It will be a safe place for you to heal and allow God to restore you." From that moment on I was hooked.

Looking back at that moment it is now easy for me to see that God was at work. I had been risking everything and expecting another defeat. I did this just so I could blame God for the crazy choices I had been making. That is really what this chapter and acronym is all about. It is time that we understood that everything Jesus did for us in human form was a tremendous risk for him.

He left heaven as a supreme deity and appeared on this earth not just as a human, but also as a human baby. And since He was fully God, while at the same time being fully human, He knew it would be extremely difficult revealing to us who He really was. He was asking humanity to risk trusting in His claims to be the Son of God. He did this so that He could bring us back into a right relationship with God the Father. He was asking us to become involved in something bigger than ourselves.

Involving yourself in something bigger than you is not a new idea or concept. It also is generally not all that difficult. We do it every day. The only difference is we tend to involve ourselves in other people's business. We also tend to do this, whether they want us to or not. Why then is it difficult to involve ourselves in things that offer us huge potential gain? After all, we will do so, with no promise of gain all the time.

I believe this goes back to the garden where we lost our involvement with God in the first place. We were humiliated and sent away from the only home we had ever known. We were walking and talking with God on a daily basis. The fall reminded us that we were not good enough to fellowship with Him. A price had to be paid just for us to receive His forgiveness.

Being a part of creation, we longed for fellowship with the Creator. When that was not realized, we turned to substitutes. But, a substitute is never as good as the real thing, no matter how good it may look, sound, taste, smell or feel. We have a natural desire to be part of something that is much greater than ourselves. And that feeling is most satisfied in a relationship. But, I'm not talking about just any relationship. We needed a lasting and longing relationship with the Almighty God of the universe.

Life-controlling problems will enter into our lives in the form of many things. Such as habits, substances or emotional bondages.

When this happens, it tends to isolate us from those we care about most. In short, our attitude becomes selfish. We live for the moment to meet our own desires. We take from whomever we want to perpetuate our lifestyle of selfishness. All the while we say we are doing it in the name of being true to our own self. Nothing could ever be further from the truth.

You and I were created to be involved in something bigger than any of us could ever imagine. So, when we lose sight of that, we are lowered to nothing more than a toy in the Devil's playground. We are then discarded like a cardboard box when he finds a new one. Being involved in something bigger than yourself will take you out of your comfort zone. Not only that but your religious zone, or any other zone you may be stuck in.

In order for people to want to change, they need to experience a pain that is greater than the pain of change. That is when you are ready to get involved. You are at the place when nothing else matters and all you want is relief. And lasting relief can only come through allowing God to be involved in taking control of your life.

Our very existence is meant to be an involvement of joy. First, it is for our Creator, and then for us. But all too often, we choose to risk our souls in the attitude of serving ourselves for a moment of pleasure. We would rather do that than risk taking a chance on a new way of life that promises us freedom.

This is true, even if it is from the hell that has become our constant companion. If that offends you then one of two things is in control of your life. Either you do not have enough pain in your life to want to change. Or you are too religious to be of help to anyone.

Serving others without respect is something that most of us do every day. We do it without even thinking about it when it comes to our family and friends. There are times, more often than we like to admit, that it's all about us. Everything we are doing is for one thing, self-gratification.

Some of us are rather good at making it appear as if we are helping other people. When, in fact, we are so busy manipulating and lying, that we begin to believe what we are telling everybody.

Even those of us that are supposedly well intentioned, have something to hide. I know what you're thinking to yourself right now. "Not me, I go to church every time the doors are open. I never miss an opportunity to help someone without expecting anything in return."

I used to be one of those people. I would work my little heart out trying to help as many people as I could. All, so that I might get my name called out from the pulpit. Or at the very least, strain my arm while trying to pat myself on the back for some good deed I had done. I remember one time when I was out until four A.M. looking for a wayward member of the singles group I was leading. I told myself I was being a good lay pastor. I was going out and looking for that one lost sheep. But the reality of it was I was looking for another color to put in my coat of many colors so that all could see what I had done.

I know, some of you are asking what does this have to do with addictions or life-controlling problems. The answer is that addictions or whatever you want to call them are selfish. The attitude of an addict is, Hey, what's in it for me?" or "When will I be able to get my next fix?"

In fact, when you think about it, this is what a lot of us like to do. I know, we change the vocabulary in order to justify it. We say things like, "I am storing up riches in heaven." or "I am trying to help people so I can get more jewels in my crown." Or my favorite one is this. "We need to pray for Sister Sally's son. He's out on a binge again and this time he took her whole Social Security check."

Let me ask you a question; when was the last time you did something without expecting anything in return? Or better yet, here's another question. When was the last time you helped someone, knowing fully well, they were using you, but you did it anyway?

That is what serving without respect means. It doesn't matter what you can do for me or for that matter what you do to me. I have decided to serve you anyway. People think I'm crazy when they find out what I do for a living. I am able to do the things I do because I have come to the conclusion that people are going to use me. And I'm okay with that.

I'm OK with that, because all the while I am being used I am taking advantage of something myself. I'm taking advantage of every opportunity to serve them. And, I'm doing this without respect to who they are or what they can do for me. I am serving them based on the fact that God sees potential in them. I am also teaching them the importance of serving others without expecting anything in return. And that leads us to the last principle of **R.I.S.K.**...

Killing. I'm specifically talking about all negative self-talk, against others or myself. I would love to be able to tell you that this is an absolute virtue of mine. But, I must admit that I am human and I fall into this trap the same as everybody else. The only hope I have is that I have learned to recognize it and try to stop it, sometimes even before it starts. This is an important principle because our words are very important. In Proverbs 18:21 we are told; "*Death and life are in the power of the tongue, and those who love it will eat its fruit.*" Then, Jesus tells his disciples something similar in in Mark 11:23. He says that whosoever; "*believes that what he says is going to happen, it will be granted him.*"

Why are words so important? It is all about physics. Spoken words become sound waves. These sound waves stay around for a long time. We send sound waves across great distances from a radio tower to the antenna in our car. We even send sound waves into outer space hoping to make contact with ET.

So, when you speak out negative words against yourself or someone else, here is what happens. They become sound waves that float around from now until all eternity. This is also the reason I'm not too fond of someone claiming to be stuck in their addictions by their words. I'm sure you know what's coming next; "Hi, my name is Mike and I'm an alcoholic or an addict." I think you're getting the picture I'm trying to paint here. We'll talk more about this as part of another chapter.

I guess right about now some of you are saying, "Oh no, he

didn't go there." To that I reply, "Oh yes I did." Others are probably saying, "What gives you the right to make that statement?" My answer is as simple as a Bible verse that can be found in Philippians 3:13-14. In this particular verse, the Apostle Paul has this to say. *"...forgetting what lies behind and reaching forward to what lies ahead, I press on toward the goal for the prize for the upward call of God in Christ Jesus."*

Paul didn't forget what he had been redeemed from. But neither did he live in the mistakes of his past. He knew where he came from. What is more important is that he knew where he was going. Individuals who struggle with addictions and other life-controlling problems already know what their issues are. They don't need to be reminded about that. They don't need to be talked about or made fun of. They need to get a glimpse of who God created them to be. They need to see themselves as God sees them. If a person can ever get a glimpse of that then they will never be the same person again.

Conclusion

Maybe you are starting to think you might have a problem and you want out of this madness. You're tired of making excuses to your loved ones for your self-damaging and self-destructive behavior and habits. You're tired of your life being so out of control. You're tired of the emotional roller coaster you find yourself on. Always going up and then down and back and forth with no end in sight. You're tired of being sick and tired whenever you are not self-medicating yourself. You're tired of feeling shame whenever you give in to your uncontrollable cravings. You're tired of being overwhelmed. You are finding it too difficult to concentrate at work, home, or school.

You're tired of being out of touch with everything that you hold dear and important in your life. You're tired of being consumed by the constant thoughts of; "How long until I can escape from this reality again and get some relief from this stress?" You are tired of seeing your childhood dreams fade away into nothingness. Your life is passing right before your very eyes. You may even be tired of

47

life itself. This is definitely not the life you dreamed of having. This is also not the happily ever after kind of future you had hoped for.

Have you ever stopped to ponder the reason why you are like this? Why you decided to let addictions take control of your life? Do you even think about the cost of all this? Or have you, like countless others, reached the point of no return? You just don't care what people think about you anymore.

Maybe you have not yet come to the conclusion that you have a problem. It could be that you've decided this is your way of coming to terms with stress. This is how you have learned to deal with things on a regular basis. The simple truth is that people get caught up in their addictions because the drugs make them feel good and forget. Even if that feeling is only for a short amount of time.

Drugs, in general, can help you cope in a lot of different ways. They can make you feel peaceful and increase your energy level. They can help you conquer social anxiety, and evade feelings of isolation. Drugs can also make you daring and cause you to take risks that endanger yourself in ways you normally would not do. They are even used to help you fit in socially and to have a good time in various party events.

Regardless of whatever your reasons may have been for using drugs, it's time to stop. It is now time to create a new outlook on life for yourself. Since you are continuing to read this far into the book. I am here to tell you there is hope. You can transform your thinking and start a new life. All you have to do is surrender your heart to God. He will help you with the rest.

It is as simple as asking Jesus to take control of your life. Right here right now, in the privacy of your own home or wherever you may be reading this book. Just pray this simple prayer with me; "Jesus, I ask to forgive me of all my sins and to take control of my life. I am tired of trying to do it on my own and am now ready to turn it over completely to you. I am ready for Your SOULUTION!"

FOOTNOTES

---

[1] *In the Shadow of the Almighty,* Elliott, Elizabeth. (Harper & Row, (c) 1958), page 108.

[2] Advanced Life Skills, Belief Systems – Part 1. Wells, Jonathan; http://advancedlifeskills.com/blog/belief-systems-part-1/

[3] https://gadelali.wordpress.com/2011/08/21/god-does-not-call-the-qualified-god-qualifies-the-called/. Accessed 9/24/15.

[4] **Modern Language Association (MLA):** "risk." *Dictionary.com Unabridged (v 1.1).* Random House, Inc. 30 Apr. 2009. <Dictionary.com http://dictionary.reference.com/browse/risk>.

M.A.P. Your SOULUTION

Make a Plan
- Write down on a piece of paper what you believe are your faulty belief systems that ultimately led you to where you are today. (Ex: *"I will never amount to anything."*) Next to each one you come up with, write why you believe you allowed yourself to buy into the faulty belief system. (Ex: *"This was spoken to me by my mother."*)
- On a separate piece of paper, write out your new belief systems based upon the truth of God's Word and what kind of person you want to be. Next to each one you come up with write how you plan on making this happen in your life.

Accept Accountability {Recruit Partner(s) to Keep You Focused}
- Pick two or three people that you believe have integrity that will meet with you weekly to work on the above.
- If it is only one for now, that is okay. Just try to reach out to more people to help you as you complete this course.

Put it into Action
- Once you and your partner(s) have come up with a plan, break it down into smaller goals you can accomplish on a daily basis.
- With your accountability, come up with deadlines on what goals are to be accomplished by what dates.

NOTES

NOTES

CHAPTER 2
OPTIMIZE

Hang on to Your H.O.P.E.

"Hope itself is like a star – not to be seen in the sunshine of prosperity, and only to be discovered in the night of adversity."
— *Charles H. Spurgeon[1]*

Ashley was one of those statistics you read about. She came to us about ten years ago. She was lost and addicted to marijuana and crystal meth. She grew up in a broken home where it was a common occurrence to see her parents and older brother on drugs. So it was no surprise when her mother got arrested and went to prison when she was only eleven years old. It was at this point that her grandmother stepped in and adopted her and two younger brothers.

Ashley was one of those statistics you read about. She came to us about ten years ago. She was lost and addicted to marijuana and crystal meth. She grew up in a broken home where it was a common occurrence to see her parents and older brother on drugs. So it was no surprise when her mother got arrested and went to prison when she was only eleven years old. It was at this point that her grandmother stepped in and adopted her and her two younger brothers.

Life was a struggle for Ashley. She was having trouble concentrating in school because of all her responsibilities at home. She had taken care of the house while her grandmother worked to support the family. She also had the added burden of making sure her two younger brothers were taken care of. This led her into a deep depression where she became lost and addicted to drugs. This lifestyle soon warped thinking. She realized she couldn't continue living like this. She took the only way out she could understand. So, at the age of sixteen, she ran away from home.

Over the course of the next year and a half Ashley found herself using drugs. At first, it was just with her dad. Then, she began hanging out with the wrong crowd. Before long, she was lost even more than before she ran away.

Ashley sensed a longing in her heart that there was more to life than living it this way. But, her life had become so complicated and confusing. She had heard about Jesus, but never knew what it meant to have a personal relationship with Him. In spite of this she would find herself crying out and praying to God in her quiet times of reflection. She even began to read the Bible in a desperate attempt to search for answers. As she would read the Bible and pray she began to strongly feel His presence. Even in the midst of her sin, she could feel God. She even sensed that He was actually real and interested in her life.

But then the unimaginable happened. Her grandmother, who had been her rock and stability, passed away. Things turned out to be very difficult from that point forward. She started having problems living at her dad's house. This led her to being semi-homeless. She would couch surf between different friends' houses.

One night, while she was at a friend's house, channel surfing. She came across the Dream Center show on Trinity Broadcasting Network (TBN). On the show was a girl who was sharing her testimony and it genuinely moved Ashley to tears. She started thinking to herself. "If the Lord could help this girl through her hurts, pains and addictions, then maybe God could help me too."

She strongly felt this was the place she was looking for. This was where she could finally experience complete healing and deliverance. So she contacted us. At that time she was not quite eighteen yet, so she couldn't come in. She had to wait a month later until her birthday, before she could come in. And, just one day after her eighteenth birthday, she started her new life by coming into the program.

While in the program she began to experience the freshness of God's grace and mercy. Day by day God was healing her from every hurt, every pain, and every addiction. Ashley flourished in the program and God granted her favor. In no time at all she was graduating from the program and then made a decision to stay a second year.

During her time with us she was able to get her GED and her driver's license as well. After finishing her second year, she became part of our volunteer program. She volunteered in various positions that enabled her to receive hands on training. She gained valuable work experience in many different areas across the campus. She even wound being the church secretary at Angelus Temple. She also served in several ministries. This included; Adopt-A-Block, the Food Truck, Skid Row Outreach, and even in the Women's Discipleship program.

In 2006 Ashley met and fell in love with the man God had destined for her. They married a couple of years later and moved away to be in full-time ministry. Today Ashley has the family she never dreamed possible. She has a loving husband and two beautiful children. She and her husband served faithfully were they were planted. And now God has birthed in them a desire to help others just as Ashley has been helped.

With that in mind they started a Dream Center with a women's recovery home soon to follow. In their local town they are living a life of success that few have ever dreamed of. Maybe not according to the world's view of success, which says, get to the top and any cost. But she is definitely one according to God's view of success of knowing God and making Him known.

Just like Ashley, we were created to reach for the stars. We were made to have H.O.P.E. What is H.O.P.E.? It is an acronym I have created to help me remember how to overcome setbacks that life may throw my way. It is one of my SOULUTIONS for life. It stands for obtaining; **H**appiness, **O**ptimism, **P**assion, & **E**xcellence in your life. I hope you find your H.O.P.E. as you journey toward your destiny.

Optimize Your Happiness

Knowing God and seeing ourselves as He sees us can be a difficult process. There are a lot of layers that have to be peeled back to get to that image. But, God placed this image there before you were even born. Now, to make matters even worse, it seems as if we are living in a perpetual Déjà vu moment. The past seems to keep repeating itself over and over again. We have trouble seeing this image God created us to be.

The keys to happiness are not given on a silver platter. Neither do they involve performing a series of steps that have to be repeated over and over again. Steps like that are designed to forever chain you to those steps. But, true happiness, can only be found in making a permanent lifestyle change. We are creatures of habit. Because of this, we tend to get comfortable in doing the same thing over and over again.

The thing is, we can get stuck in a rut when we keep repeating the same thing, over and over again. When we get stuck in one of these bad habits, it creates a vortex. This will then send a person further and further down into a deep, dark, abyss with no point of return. When this happens to us we sometimes just tend to give up. It is easier to go with the flow, thinking that we are destined to live that way until we die.

But, God never intended for us to live this way. Jesus himself said something powerful in John 10:10. He said; *"The thief comes only to steal and kill and destroy, I am came that they may have life, and have it abundantly."* Not just a life that consists of three hot's and a cot. That's three square meals and a bed to those of you not in the recovery field. He also came to give us a plentiful life.

A life that is so awesome it is overflowing with joy and happiness. He came to give us a life that he created just for us. God knew that in this life we would have hardships. That is why God came down in the form of the man Jesus, to show us how to overcome these adversities in life. And if the truth were known, it is this. That we already have the power to get out of the rut we have become stuck in. We just have to realize we were created for this moment.

There is a very powerful story in the Bible about Queen Esther. She had won a beauty pageant over the whole known world at that time to become queen. Can you imagine how happy she must have been? A few years after that, her people, the Jews were in danger of being wiped out. It was then up to her to try and do something to prevent it from happening. It was a hard decision for her to make. She really was reluctant to do it for fear of losing her life if the plea failed.

But in the end, her uncle convinced her that this was her destiny. He spoke those famous words that have been used many times to inspire greatness, from Esther 4:14. *"For if you remain silent at this time, relief and deliverance will arise for the Jews from another other place and you and your father's house will perish. And who knows whether you have not attained royalty for such a time as this?"*

The wonderful thing about this story is that it is not just Esther's story. It is my story, it is your story, and it's the story of that loved one that so desperately wants to be restored. We all were on the verge of destruction, whether drugs or stupidity or both. The end result is still the same.

But God has taken the adversity and turned it inside out to make it a doorway to freedom and happiness. Determination and commitment are what is needed right now. That is what will enable you to discover the joy and happiness God has placed inside each and everyone one of us. No matter how far away we may have drifted from Him, He is still there waiting for us to call on Him for help.

What is it that makes you happy? Genuine happiness is not based on outside influences and circumstances. It is based on a joy that starts on the inside and works its way to an outward manifestation in your life. So knowing this, I want to ask you again. What makes you happy?

I would like to ask you to get a paper and something to write with right now. Draw a line down the center of the page from top to bottom. On the left hand side, at the top of the paper, write "Things That Steal My Happiness". Now on the right hand side, at the top of the paper, write "Things That Make Me Happy". Now, stop reading and take some time to make a list. Make sure you put at least five in each column.

Now that you are finished go back and look over your list. Go through each item on the list and determine which things on the list are things that you have control over. Circle these with your pen. These are the things that you can do something about right now. Now you know how to hold on to the things that make you happy. You also know how to avoid the things that can steal your happiness.

No doubt, there will be items left on both sides of your list. These are things of which you do not have control over. You may want to look over them one more time just to be sure you have no control over them. If you think you do then once again circle them. If not, you are now ready for a major revelation.

The things that are left on this list are not dependent upon you. You have no control over them. Therefore, you can do nothing about them. So you now have two choices. You can 1) Stop letting them bother you because you have no control over them. Or 2) Figure out the steps you need to take to resolve each of these items. Either way, you win! You now know how to hold on to your happiness.

Optimize Your Outlook

Uncharted territory is a scary place to be in. We are putting everything at risk just to; "...boldly go where no man has gone before[2]..." Okay, I know it's a little cheesy but I love Star Trek. The whole show is about taking risks by going to places that nobody has ever seen or been to before.

I know right now, some of you are reading this book because you want a quick fix. Something frightening may have just happened to you and you are seeking answers. If that is you, then I imagine you're pretty confused right about now. You need immediate help with your problems and you are wondering what all this stuff has to do with you. Right? Remember the beginning of my story I started in chapter one? Let's get back to it now.

Okay, so I had bared my soul to a complete stranger and started going to church there. I'd love to tell you that everything was perfect and my upside down life was turned right side up again. There is a saying that I heard growing up. It is basically, a sarcastic way to make light of difficult situation. My friends and I used it a lot whenever we wanted something good to happen. Yet deep down inside we knew that it was very unlikely. Are you ready for it? Here it is; "Ain't gonna happen".

This is real life we're talking about here. While telling someone my troubles was a start to my healing process, it didn't solve ANY of my problems. They were still there because change is a process. And believe me, it was definitely a process to change the mess I found myself in. There were no overnight answers for me.

It never ceases to amaze me that we humans can be so impatient when it comes to demanding answers to our problems. As the saying goes, "Rome wasn't built in a day." I had to learn how to be optimistic. And given what I was feeling at the time, I didn't see that happening for a long time. The thought of more pain bummed me out even more.

Consider something with me for a moment. We will spend years shoveling fast food into our bodies and developing unhealthy habits. Then, when we get an unsettling report from our doctor, we expect God to heal our bodies overnight. We will also spend many years getting into tens of thousands of dollars worth of debt. And then, some financial unexpected emergency occurs. As a result of this, we expect God to give us the winning numbers to the next million-dollar lottery ticket. All in the name of favor so we can magically get out of debt.

I for one, must confess that most of the time, I am guilty of this type of self-defeating mindset. It is, only when I surround myself with accountability, that I begin to see what my part of the

SOULUTION is. This same line of faulty thinking seems to exist among most people.

If you are struggling with addictions and other problems, it may be the same for you. No matter how many years you have been involved in this lifestyle, you are not the exception to the rule. You are expecting God to wave His magic wand of sobriety and make it all go away without much effort. "Ain't gonna happen!"

I was recently at a faith-based addiction conference that made a point about this belief. The speaker brought up the fact that most people raised around Christianity, think the same thing. They believe that by crying out to God, they can be instantly delivered from whatever habits they are bound to. The laws of Seed, Plant, and Harvest, do not apply to them.

He then went on to say that in reality, only two to four per cent of these people are actually instantly delivered. The rest have to go through a process. H.O.P.E. doesn't always happen overnight. So don't give up. Keep on hoping because it is a process that builds your faith.

Anyway, back to my story. I soon realized that God loved me for who I was. Not for whom I was married to or what denomination I belonged to. He, the Everlasting God of all creation loved spending time with me, just because. To make a long story short, I got back in ministry again with that church as the Singles Pastor.

Everything seemed to be going great. Life was great. I had joint custody of my daughter. Living out my dreams of being back in ministry. I even met another woman who would eventually become my second wife. But something was happening to me that I failed to notice. I was falling back into my old rut again. I was becoming religious. Going through the motions, "having a form of godliness but denying the power."

Limitations have always been something that I have struggled with. Whether they are self imposed or set up by someone else. I didn't realize at first, that I was struggling, but God did, and He understood. He knew I was human. Besides, I was doing a wonderful ministry. I was ministering to hurting single adults and teaching divorce recovery classes.

By this time I was married and the honeymoon was wearing off. Our church was going through the *Prayer of Jabez,* and at times, it became difficult. I couldn't understand what was happening. I was praying for God to enlarge my territory but I kept running into all these walls. What I didn't understand at the time was that growth was a painful process. In order for God to enlarge my territory and bear more fruit. I had to experience some pruning and the growing pains that came with it. And believe me, there was a lot of growing to come.

"We missed the will of God in getting married so the only thing to do is end it." Those words slapped me in the face on that fateful day as they came out of my wife's mouth. I couldn't believe what I was hearing. The only thing more hurtful than going through a divorce was to go through another divorce.

A lot of things were going through my mind. How could she think God would ever want something like that to happen? I must confess that my next thought was not very spiritual. All I could think about was what was going to happen to my ministry? Then, deep despair began to settle down over me. I realized that my life in ministry was over.

Who would ever want a two-time loser to minister to their congregation? To make matters worse, the church finally had enough income to hire an associate pastor. My pastor and I had strategized over lunch many times as to how we could grow the congregation. Our plan was for the church to grow so that it could afford to put me on staff. And now that it was within reach, I watched it slip through my fingers. Because of my divorce, someone else filled the position that I felt, belonged to me.

My world was falling apart. My pastor even came and had lunch with me to tell me the news. It was surreal. It was like an out of body experience. I was there, but yet I wasn't. He kept telling me that he wouldn't blame me if I wanted to go to another church in light of what was happening.

As we ended the meeting it was as if he was saying goodbye to me. As I got out of his car that day his words still echo in my mind. "Man, I'm sorry things didn't work out. I hope you have a nice life." I walked inside the building in a daze. I was in shock at what had just transpired. I felt as if my Pastor, my friend was giving up on me. All I could think of at the time was that my life was anything besides nice.

Here I was again. I was confused and lost. I didn't even know which way was up. Then I remembered an old friend who had moved back into the state a few years back. He was now, ironically pastoring the church I used to attend when I went through my first divorce. I cannot stress enough that I was more than a little mad at God for allowing all this to happen. How could He have deserted me in my deepest, darkest hours?

I would love to say that at that moment I returned to my "roots" if you would. And, that everything in my world begin to right itself and my positivity returned. But it did not! In fact, there were still a lot of dark days ahead of me as I walked through my desert. But, I came to understand that this was all part of something much greater than myself. God was preparing me to minister to people who were marching across their own desert. They needed help to find their oasis in the midst of the hell they had found themselves trapped in.

What is it that you have H.O.P.E. for? Write it down and keep it taped up somewhere visible so that you can see it every single day. Someplace, like the mirror, where you get ready each morning. You need this to keep your spirit alive. This will help you see the big picture that God has for you. It will also help you hold on to your assurance that God still loves you and is looking out for you.

Optimize Your Passion

Tom Jones is one of those rare men that that God placed in my life. He has an uncanny ability to be your best friend and worst antagonist at the same time. I love that man like my own brother. But, I have learned not to ask his opinion unless I am ready to hear the truth and be challenged. We have known each other for nearly forty years. So he knows me better than most. I say that, even though we haven't spent a lot of those years together. We have a kindred spirit that wants to see hurting souls delivered and set free from the bondages of hell.

By the time of my second divorce I was working in a homeless shelter. I was the Operations Director for The City Rescue Mission in downtown Oklahoma City. It seemed as if I had finally found my passion and purpose in life. Helping hurting men and women recover their lives from the path of destruction.

I settled into a routine at work and was working with the church helping Tom. One day I found out that there was a team going to the Los Angeles Dream Center for a conference. The team leader approached me to see if I would be interested in going. My heart leaped within me. At last I was finally getting to see a place that had been in my heart for over five years.

I had discovered Pastor Tommy Barnett's Conference and the Dream Center in 1997. However, I left all that behind when I left the Assembly of God church after my second divorce. I had even wanted to go and visit the Los Angeles Dream Center but things never worked out.

I'll never forget that visit. I never had a desire to go to California other than to visit the Dream Center. I thought California was largely unchurched and full of hippies. I also thought there were a lot of crazy people living there. But, that all changed in the summer of 2002.

I went on an outreach to Skid Row in downtown Los Angeles. My heart was broken as I saw homeless people in tents that stretched for blocks and blocks. I secretly longed to be here and even voiced it to my daughter on the phone during a break in the conference. But, all good things must come to an end as the saying goes and at the end of the week we headed back to Oklahoma.

The irony of all this was that after my second divorce I went back to Pastor Barnett's Leadership School. I needed to find some answers and direction for my life. I remember being on the top balcony of that church and looking down. As I saw all the ministries that took place in this church. I also remember praying this prayer. "God, I know that with two divorces I will never be a Sr. Pastor. But, I would love to be on staff at a church like this, if you could make that happen?" In spite of everything that was happening in my life, I still had a passion to help hurting people. It was, I believe my purpose in life.

Let's get back to the story. I went back home and settled back into the daily routine of helping people at the shelter. I remember crying out to God one day. I told Him; "I have tried to be successful in ministry the best way that I knew how and I have failed miserably. If you want me to be here for the rest of my life pouring into these hurting men and women, then that is what I will do."

It was a simple prayer, but it was something I meant from deep inside of my heart. God heard my prayer. He honored my prayer. In March of 2003 I was asked to come on staff to be the director of the Discipleship program at The Dream Center. I am now living my dream and passion.

God is no respecter of persons. What He did for me He can and will do for you. What is your passion? What do you enjoy doing? What would you do if you could do anything in the world and not have to worry about making money? The answer to those questions is what your passion and purpose is all about. And when the two collide, great things happen that change lives.

Optimize Your Excellence

I want to take a moment and look back at Ashley's story for a minute. It took some time with her, but God was working in her life. He was at work to get her into alignment with a truly unique assignment. This was an assignment, which He had handcrafted just for her. It was like God was making all her dreams come true. By allowing her to become a part of something bigger and greater than herself, He was changing her.

After all, isn't this what really drives us? Don't we all long to be part of something bigger and better than ourselves? Something that makes us want to strive for excellence? That is what this process is all about. We all have an assignment that God has spoken into our lives from even before we were even born. The prophet Jeremiah knew this when God spoke to him in Jeremiah 1:5; *"Before I formed you in the womb I knew you, and before you were born I consecrated you; I have appointed you a prophet to the nations."*

God spoke his assignment over him before he was born. God has also spoken an assignment over you and ever since He spoke out that assignment, the Devil, the accuser of our souls, has tried to destroy you. He has set out to speak against what God has already spoken into your soul. He will do everything within his power to cause you to lose hope.

I am a firm believer that is the reason why so many people struggle with life-controlling issues. There is a huge assignment that God has for them to do as part of their assignment. But, at the same time, the enemy is out to kill, steal, and destroy you. He will do anything that he possibly can to get us out of alignment with our assignment.

Before you were a twinkle in the eyes of your parents, you were the apple of His eye. He created you for excellence and with a specific assignment He had in mind for you. Until you step into that assignment, you will not be truly fulfilled. That is why you are always looking for the next BIG thing to please you.

It is also easy to mistake your assignment with being in the limelight. In fact, one of the things we can learn from the people that God used in the Bible is this. God uses ordinary people to do extraordinary things. Sometimes, the extraordinary thing is doing the ordinary thing with excellence. When everyone else around you is searching for their fifteen minutes of fame, and taking shortcuts to get there, you must strive for excellence in everything you do.

Tom Jones, whom I previously mentioned, preached a sermon one time at Angelus Temple. It was about getting into alignment with your assignment. As a result of this sermon and my personal experiences, my life has been changed. I want to share with you what learned from that sermon.

First, your assignment is usually to a person or a group of people. There is a reason why you may feel comfortable and drawn to certain individuals or people groups. It is from God.

Second, your assignment will determine the level of attacks and suffering you will experience. In fact, the reason you may not be fully into your assignment yet is because you aren't ready. You have not been seasoned enough to handle these attacks. You must trust the process.

Third, what you love the most reveals a lot about your assignment. God doesn't make mistakes. He created you with an inescapable gifting and a passion towards certain things and circumstances. This is what keeps you focused. It is what you love and makes you happy. Enjoy this moment.

Fourth, your assignment is geographical. Where you are is just as important as what you are. You might be the biggest fish in the world, such as a gray whale. But you better make sure you are living in the ocean. If you're not, you won't survive for very long.

Fifth, your assignment has to become an obsession with you. I remember when I was a Singles Pastor in a local church and I went to see my old mentor. During our conversation he pointed out that he didn't feel I was called into that area. He said all I did was talk about how needy single people were. Years later when I started working in a homeless shelter, he reminded me of that conversation. He said that now all I talked about was how much I love my job and how it had become an obsession with me.

Sixth, your assignment will require seasons of preparation. As I look back over my life I can see how one job prepared me for the next one. Now, as I look at where I am in my life, I can see how all the other experiences have prepared me for this moment. Don't rush the season you are in. It will end when you are ready to move on to the next season God has for you.

Finally, you must never forget your assignment will always have an enemy. Ever since being kicked out of Heaven, the Devil has been going about seeking whom he may destroy. He will never stop until you are dead. Never forget this and never let your guard down. The Devil never will. He sees you not as you are, but who you are destined to be. Isn't it time you did the same?

Conclusion

In the early part of the 20th century there was an American author. His name was Napoleon Hill and he was to become one of the founding fathers of the personal success movement. His books have been influential in the success of many individuals throughout the century. Even today, his books are still being sold and read by countless individuals.

Napoleon Hill's story was truly a rags-to-riches story. His story has continued to provide motivation and encouragement to millions of people. Even though, he wrote his first book nearly a hundred years ago. I know that some of you may be asking; "What does any of this have to do with my addiction and restoration process?" The answer is, more than you think.

Now let's look a deeper look at my reasoning . Napoleon Hill was blessed to be able to speak to some of the most powerful and successful people of his time. He spent twenty years doing research for his book. During that time he questioned the wealthiest and most powerful people around the world.

The purpose of his book was to find out what made these individuals so successful. As a result of these interviews, he was able to come up with a specific set of strategies for success. He had discovered what all these people had in common with each other. They all had a plan for what they wanted to do. And, they were willing to stick with that plan, until they had accomplished their goals.

This conviction can be incredibly decisive in overcoming any setbacks you face in life. The strategy for this is quite simple. We have to know where we are going into truly get there. This is also evident in many ancient and wise sayings. The book of Proverbs is one such book where we can read one of these sayings. In chapter twenty-three and the first part of verse seven it says this. "*Hope deferred makes the heart sick, but when the desire comes, it is a tree of life."* NKJV

In order to have H.O.P.E. and be successful at anything, you must have a plan. This is especially important when it comes to your recovery. You must structure a plan for realizing your H.O.P.E. Without a purpose and a plan to get to your destination, you will wander around without direction. It has even been said that if you fail to plan then you are making a plan to fail.

So the real question is not; what does this have to do with me but how can I make this SOULUTION work for me? Many people have started on the road to restoration, only to fail. They encountered roadblocks in their search for success. But, because they had a plan, or SOULUTION, they got back on course. It is my hope and prayer that as you encounter these roadblocks, that you stick with the SOULUTIONS contained in this book and not turn back. For that is the way to hold on to your H.O.P.E. that God has for you.

FOOTNOTES

[1] Spurgeon, C. (n.d.). Hope. . Retrieved July 10, 2014, from http://www.goodreads.com/quotes/search?utf8=✓&q=hope%2C+spurgeon&commit=Search

[2] Roddenberry, G. (2011, March 20). Is the "Space, The Final Frontier" quote "in universe"?. . Retrieved July 10, 2014, from http://scifi.stackexchange.com/questions/2545/is-the-space-the-final-frontier-quote-in-universe

M.A.P. Your SOULUTION

Make a Plan
- Take some time after reading this chapter to reflect upon what your **H.O.P.E.** is based on. Now get a piece of paper and write down what were some things that may have caused you to lose your hope. Be specific honest as you possibly can.
- Next, write out some new hopes that are just now beginning to surface in the back of your mind. It is important that you cultivate these and water them with encouragement from yourself and others that you trust.

Accept Accountability {Recruit Partner(s) to Keep You Focused}
- Set down with your partner(s) to brainstorm and try to determine the first time you lost hope.
- Next, determine how they can give hope to you when they sense you becoming a little hopeless.

Put it into Action
- Make it a point this week to go out this week and offer hope to some hopeless individuals you may come across. You will be surprised and how contagious hope can be. It can be as simple as giving a flower to a homeless person as you give him your spare change.

NOTES

NOTES

CHAPTER 3

UNCOVER

Realize Your Revelation

"Where there is no revelation, the people cast of restraint..."
Proverbs 29:18a NKJV

Erin had a childhood love for God. She understood that God knew her by name. He was interested in her even before the moment she walked down the aisle to surrender her life to Christ. It happened during a children's gathering. It was like the whole room stood still while God spoke into her heart and said she was important to Him.

This was the beginning of her journey that would show God's amazing power and love in her young life. As Erin grew up she developed a fearless sense of adventure. Unfortunately it was salted with unbridled rebellious attitude. She lacked common sense, respect for life, or any kind of order or discipline. She continued to grow and explore all life had to offer. To say that she became a handful for her parents is an understatement.

As soon as Erin started High School she soon realized how much drugs and alcohol would change her life. In her own words she had this to say; "It was like I became this really cool person and could live outside of myself." She got involved in the party scene and partied throughout High School. She was drinking and drugging at any opportunity. Her whole motive was just to have a good time and feel free.

She lived her life by a different reasoning. She thought it was foolish to get caught up in doing stuff she was supposed to do. Why would she want to do that? She could just party all the time and do whatever her heart desired. This course of action led to her getting alcohol poisoning at the age of sixteen.

Needless to say, her parents didn't approve of her behavior. This led to many arguments as well as a lot of strife in the house. The home became completely divided with constant arguing, yelling. She would be grounded, time and time again. The police where even called on occasion when things went too far. So it wasn't much of a surprise when after graduating High School Erin moved out on her own.

Over the span of five years Erin lived her life as the scripture says in James 1:13-15 NKJV. *"Let no one say, when he is tempted, 'I am tempted by God.'; for God cannot be tempted by evil, nor does He Himself tempt anyone. But each one is tempted when he is drawn away by his own desires and enticed. Then, when desire is conceived, it gives birth to sin; and sin, when it is full-grown, brings forth death."* She was living her life according to the principle of "Whatever feels good, do it!" This opened the door to death and destruction for her. Her life was turned into a living, hellish nightmare on earth.

Erin had a lot of wake up calls that she never took heed to. There were so many countless stories of God's protection in her life. The power of freedom, she had sought after for so long, became an addiction that enslaved her. It took away all her dignity. Her addictions stripped her of everything she had. She lost all her material possessions, her family, and even her desire to live.

She wandered the streets for days on end. She had been arrested and put in jails where she would wake up and not know where she was. A group of firefighters once woke her up downtown, just to make sure she was still alive. She has taken enough drugs to kill a grown man. Yet despite all this, her life was somehow miraculously spared.

Then one day, in a final attempt of determination. She decided to purchase a "one-way ticket to forgetfulness" as she called it, in her own words. Traveling with some bags, a wad of cash, and a rock (crack-cocaine) half the size of her hand, she was off to nowhere. She was hoping to end her nightmare once and for all. She was completely empty with no feelings left.

Revelation came to Erin through a series of events that she believed were God-inspired. During her "one-way ticket to forgetfulness" something happened. Her eyes became open to the spiritual realm. This occurred through witchcraft and Satanism, which had surrounded her. This experience brought her to a face-off, eye-to-eye with the Devil. It was in that very moment she realized who she was. And, it was that knowledge that completely changed her. A righteous anger began to consume within her. Scriptures from childhood memories began to spew out of her mouth. She began proclaiming God's authority and victory over evil.

Erin immediately threw away her drugs along with the desire for them. She never wanted to touch them again. That moment also left her with a fervent hatred for evil and the desire to expose it to everyone. Yet, something within her knew that God didn't want her preaching tweaker-twisted gospel. God was willing to accept her for who she was, but was she willing to accept this new lifestyle? She understood that she needed help, and that help came in the form of coming into our program.

She realized that she had to consecrate her life to the Word of God. His power was the only possible method that would change her into the person she was destined to become. The SOULUTION of using a revelation of the Word of God spoke to her soul. In order to overcome life-controlling problems, truth had to be revealed to her. This was the only thing that brought her back to a functional state of mind.

Her struggles are not over, but they definitely are fewer and she now has the tools she needs to overcome them. Since completing the program, Erin has turned her life around. She has learned to deal with her own failures and disappointments. But she has also learned to accept the fact that

God is working in her. He is giving her the desire to obey Him, and the power to do what pleases Him. That basically means that she doesn't have to worry about her abilities or lack of them. She has learned to just trust in the Lord because He is the only one that has the power to change her.

Uncover Your Dreams

It never rains in Southern California. At least that's what the song says. I guess that's part of the appeal of this place. There are beautiful people, beautiful weather, all living a beautiful life. But I think you are smart enough to know, this is not the case.

There is no such thing as Paradise, this side of Heaven. And, more often than not, your dreams can, and will come crashing down around you. It will happen regardless of what side of the railroad tracks you grow up on. It doesn't matter who your daddy is, or what color of skin you have.

Eventually the rain stops and the sun will ever so slightly begin to peek through the clouds. It is always better after the rain. The skies are clear. The air is fresh. It seems as if God has just hit the reset button for the day.

Life is a lot like that. There are times when it seems as if everything is blurry. Kind of like, looking at life through the falling rain. But then; the rain stops, the clouds clear and we see things clearly once again.

In Los Angeles, where I live, the air can become quite hazy from all the smog. Sometimes it is hard to even see a mountain next to the freeway you are traveling on. But after a good rain you can see around the area for miles and miles all because the rain has cleaned the air.

Sometimes things can happen in our lives that aren't what we wanted or even planned to happen. And it can create a cloud or even rain in our life. But, given time, the clouds will clear. And, we will come to our senses, because now, we can see much clearer.

The reason I'm using this analogy for you is because I know people. It would be nice to think you got this book because you were highly motivated to change. And, that you're not going to let anything stop you or get in your way. But I am a realist, and I get it that many of you will start this book but never finish it.

There may be some of you that will start it, but then, lose interest and put it away. Then after a storm in your life clears up, and you are thinking with a clear head, you will pick it back up again. But you know what, that's OK. You have to want to change. It doesn't come from wishful thinking or as a result of an accident. You have to see where you are, where you want to be, and what it will take for you to get there. No one else can do it for you.

It would be great if I could tell you there were some simple magic formula that would get you there overnight. But there isn't anything like that. It takes hard work, just like anything in life, for you to make some great desire come to pass. And, if there were some shortcut, it wouldn't be as effective at keeping you there, would it?

There is something you can do. You can grasp hold of the fact that you need help. Erin's story is typical of many individuals that have experienced their own revelation. They have learned this by using the SOULUTIONS they have found within the pages of the Bible. These are people who are desperate to see hope beyond their own circumstances.

It's as though they can't see straight. Their dream has somehow gotten blurred. They need help in seeing this again. They need to rescue their dreams. And to do that, you must have a radical revelation of whom you are and what you were meant to do in your life.

So, I know some of you may be asking; "What exactly is a radical revelation and what does that look like?" For some of you it brings up thoughts of the end times as seen by the Apostle John in the book of Revelation.

When I think about what a radical revelation means to me, I see myself living a life beyond anything I ever dreamed of. A life full of adventures, in doing things that is bigger than my abilities. I see this for me, in spite of what others may think. That is a radical revelation.

Obviously, in the light of scriptures, we must see ourselves the way God sees us. For instance, God tells us He knows our thoughts and intentions and looks at the heart, or inside. Man, on the other hand, tends to only see from the outside. God also tells us that He has a plan and a future for us, if we will submit to His will. But then, that is where the confusion sets in, doesn't it? Just how do we figure out what exactly God's will is?

Another insight into all this is figuring out what do you want. What is your dream? I will even go so far to say that is even harder than figuring out what God wants. But in reality, I believe they are both more closely related than we could ever imagine. God has given us the desires of our heart. Desires, that have been placed deep within us, to lead us to our destiny.

From the verse at the beginning of this chapter it would be easy to assume that two things are important in life. One, we must have a dream of something that is beyond our abilities. And two, this dream is what will keep us going forward as long as we don't lose sight of it (cast off restraint).

So now, the question then becomes; how do we do this? How can we bring these two things together so that we won't cast off the mental sight of our vision, dream, or desire? Just how do we become free from the life-controlling problems we have found ourselves in? This is the stuff dreams are made of. So, let's continue look at this idea a little closer.

Uncover Your Senses

Have you ever been to a 3-D movie? They are popular right now. You are given a pair of glasses that enables you to see the special effects. In fact, if you take off the glasses and try to watch the movie without them it is an unpleasant experience. It is very frustrating to your eyes.

One of the things that stand out to me, when it comes to substance abuse is this. We have a hard time seeing ourselves as other people see us. And I'm not talking about a good way. I call this the "3-D Vision Syndrome". It's really, a simple concept.

Someone, who is an addicted person, will

sometimes see himself or herself in this way. Their life is not so clear. As a result of this, they have to put on these special glasses in order to see themselves in a different light. Those glasses are the substances they are using. Other people can see the difference and realize that there is a problem here. But they are wearing their 3-D glasses and can't see it.

This condition is a gradual process and does not happen overnight. That is why we, ourselves, have a hard time believing what people are saying. We tend to look at ourselves in light of what we are experiencing. Not what other people are telling us.

For instance, at the writing of this book, I am fifty-five years old. However, in my mind, I don't think of myself as being that old. I look at the best side of myself in the light of what society considers "normal".

Nevertheless, that view of myself gets altered after a physically taxing event. Mainly, because on the day after, I wake up to a host of aches and pains. Those pains remind me that I am no longer in my twenties, thirties, or even forties for that matter.

Let me share with you how the three D's of this process works. At first you will get **D**istracted. This happens when you stop seeing yourself as God sees you. Next, you become **D**eceived. This is where you begin to believe the lie the enemy has told you about yourself. And finally, you are **D**estroyed. Everything you have ever worked hard for comes unraveled. You are living in utter destruction and chaos.

The reality of life is this. Almost everyone is addicted to something in his or her life. Take caffeine for instance. My wife used to have a sign in her office that read; "I don't have a problem with caffeine, I have a problem without it." Other addictions may include; shopping, smoking, exercise, gambling, work, etc. For most of us these habits don't cause us many concerns.

The trouble starts when it begins to control your life. You may be addicted, if, when you get up in the morning, it's the first thing on your mind. You may be in trouble if it is first in your life before anything else. You may struggle with addictions or life-controlling issues and not know it. If you find yourself missing work, family functions, or other significant activities on a regular basis, you may have a problem. You may even get to a point where you will have to have your "fix" before being able to cope with people or things.

This is particularly true with substance abuse. It becomes hazardous to yourself and to others when you find yourself "using" before work or when driving a vehicle. If you suspect this is happening to you then you may have already lost control. You have been caught in an ever-widening web of addiction. Ask yourself the thought-provoking questions below to see where you stand.

- What troubles are you dealing with due to your drug/alcohol use?
- Are you or have you been in trouble with the law as a result of drug/alcohol use?
- Are you or have you been absent from school or work due to the use of drugs, alcohol or something else?
- Do you know how much you are actually using? Be honest for your own sake! How much money you are spending on this habit. Write it down so you can see it on paper.
- Are you or have you told lies about your "problem?"
- Are you or have you justified your use of drugs because they are prescribed to you by a Doctor?
- Are you or have you been to more than three different Doctors in the last month to get prescriptions filled?
- Are you or have you taken drugs or alcohol just to fit in?

If you answered yes to any of these questions then you might have a problem. This is a sign that it is time for you to get help. If you are tired of being sick and tired, then it's time to change! If you are tired of all the excuses you give to justify your actions, then it is time to quit!

It's important for you understand something. In order to get better, you must first rediscover your revelation of who God created you to be. This is the area most people fail at in attempting to get sober. They are just not ready to quit.

Secondly, you must make the choice to find the right SOULUTIONS that will help you in your desire to get better. Suppose you happen to be one of those select few individuals who feels like your problem is just not that bad. Or maybe, someone that cares about you is trying to force this upon you. If either of these are your reasons, you need to ask yourself why you got this book. Maybe you have some other lame reason for not wanting to do this. If that is you, then I'm going to ask just one thing from you. ***STOP READING NOW!***

I'm sorry, but at this time, you are not ready to get help. Whatever your reason for using is, it between you and God and I'm not going to force you to something you don't want to do. You have made your choice and I will be here, should you ever change your mind. For those of you still reading, great! The SOULUTIONS and strategies in this book can help you. But, before we continue any further, I want you do something for me. I want you to forget about everything you have ever heard about addiction recovery.

Forget about the advice your Uncle Joe has given you. I know, he has been in recovery for twenty-seven years and never misses a meeting. I am not saying that what Uncle Joe is doing does not work. It works for him, and some of the things may work for you as well.

I'm not going to talk about addictive personalities, genetics, or twelve steps. All this will do is suffocate your mind with information. You will hardly use it and probably don't even care about. What I am going to talk about first, is finding out whom you were meant to be, your revelation.

Uncover Your Viewpoint

I know the previous statement might seem pretty harsh to you. But it is necessary for you to have an open mind as we dig into this subject. After all, if you valued your Uncle Joe's advice, then you would not have needed this book, would you?

I will be the first to agree with you that it is important to listen to other people's sound advice. However, you need to listen most to what they are seeing in your life. Maybe there are some things they see that you do not. This is especially true if they are family or if they have known you for quite some time.

They have a genuine interest in you. They want to see you whole and transformed because they truly care about you. There is one thing that Erin learned in her journey that helped her a lot. She rediscovered a revelation of who she was. She had to learn to look beyond herself and see what other people saw in her. The secret to this is quite simple. You need to learn to see yourself through someone else's eyes. This goes both ways, for the good and the bad.

First, in order to do this, you have to take a good hard look at yourself. You must take a look in the mirror and see yourself just as you are. Without all the hype or the excuses that have come to be part of your personality. This is not an easy task and may take some time to learn to do it well enough to make a difference. But don't give up! Keep looking and you will soon uncover the real you.

Next, you must see yourself as others see you. If you could fully see the mess you have made of your life, you would want to change. If you could see it from the viewpoint of a close friend or family member, it would make a drastic impact on your life. While these two viewpoints would help, it wouldn't be all you'd need. That is what brings us to the third viewpoint.

You need to see yourself as God sees you. This is just as important as the other two. When you look at yourself in this way, you can see yourself, as you should be. You can walk in the revelation of who God created you to be. The reason you need these three viewpoints is that it represents the real you. You see the past, the missed opportunities, and the bad things that have happened to you. Other people will see the flaws in you, your mistakes and failures. They will see all the things you are not. But God sees the future in you. He sees what He created you to be.

I am not talking about being a perfect individual in every area of our life. The imperfections we have are what make us human. The potential God gives us is what allows us to hope for a better tomorrow. It is what God uses to show the world He still works miracles in people's lives. I know that some people say it's not good to have a pie in the sky type of optimism but I disagree. In fact, you just read a whole chapter about that. It costs nothing to dream but it can cost you everything if you fail to dream.

What good does looking at the past do for you? For the most part, it does absolutely nothing. However, it does accomplish one important thing. It gives you a starting point for your future. It is already done and there is nothing you can do to change it. Other people will look at you and put labels on you. But you have the ability to look to the future. You must never give up on seeing the dreams inside of you come to pass.

The Apostle Paul said this in Philippians 3:13-14. "...*forgetting what lies behind and reaching forward to what lies ahead, I press on toward the goal for the prize of the upward call of God in Christ Jesus.*" Your race is not yet over. How do I know that? If it were, you wouldn't be reading this book. You would either be dead or living a different lifestyle so as not to be in need of this book, except to help someone else.

As long as you can see the future you can have the hope of restoration. Not being recovered to where you used to be. But restored to like new condition. In fact, some of you are where you are right now because of the way things were in your life. You need to be restored back to the original "factory-like condition." The way God created you to be. To fulfill the destiny He created in you. You will never be the person you were meant to be until you find your place in His will.

Uncover Your Realization

But that is always the hard part, isn't it? It seems like most of us know what we're supposed to be doing; we just never get around to doing it. Or, we tried to do it our way, instead of the way God meant for it to happen. Come on! You know what I'm talking about.

Let's face it; you don't like doing it God's way because it's boring. You need excitement in your life. You weren't created to be dull. God has created you to be someone who is exciting and unique. He created someone that would stand out in a crowd. While all this is true to some extent, let me ask you a question? In the words of Dr. Phil; "How's that working out for you so far?"

Regardless of where you are going right now you have a choice to make. Do you continue on that path even if it is the wrong one? Or do you admit that you are traveling in the wrong direction. And better yet, will you stop and ask for help? The important thing is that you realize you need help to get to your destination.

Reality is rarely what we want it to be. In fact, reality is a harsh world of accepting the truth about us. It is also accepting the truth about others that we have put our trust in. If we are honest with ourselves, we know it is more than that. We are still struggling with life-controlling problems, so we turn to the only thing we know to be constant in our lives. Our trust is in the addictions that we have put our trust in.

You have to stop and ask yourself, "What is it that really motivates me?" For some, it is the simple pleasure of seeing life played out in front of them as a spectator. For others they can't even understand why people don't just "grab life by the horns" and "go for the gusto." To these individuals, it is all about experiencing everything that this world has to offer. These individuals live by the motto, "If it feels good do it."

Let's be honest with each other, can we? For some of you standing out in a crowd was the last time you were picked out of a police lineup. Yes, I just went there! And if you are reading this book then I think you are ready for a change. But are YOU ready for a change? If so, then hopefully you are ready to try something new. Because what I'm proposing to you is going to be like nothing you have ever encountered before. You need to discover a fresh revelation. But, a revelation which will get your attention and cause a radical shift in your reality.

Conclusion

I want you to understand one thing. I'm not going to sugar coat things for you. I think if you're still reading this book you can see that by now. There are also going to be obstacles in this new path if you choose to follow.

The biggest obstacle you are going to have to overcome is yourself. If you have gotten to a place in your life where you understand this, then you know what I'm talking about. You have to be brutally honest with yourself, if you want your freedom back. Because, the reality of all this comes down to one thing. You are the only one that can prevent YOU from getting better.

There are no doubt many reasons why Erin did the things she did. She was trying to rescue her revelation and fight for freedom. Hopefully, the same can happen to you. Maybe, some of the reasons listed in the following chapters will be able to help you on your pathway to peace.

You must develop a steadfast mindset that nothing will stop you. You must believe that nothing is going to prevent you from reaching your potential. The story of Erin is a moving and powerful illustration. It is the story of an individual coming face to face with her pain and trying to realize why this is happening to her. Just as Erin changed, you too, can change. But it will only happen if you realize the truth and allow God to do what He has been trying to do to you your whole life. You must learn to believe in yourself again.

Believing in yourself is harder to do than most people can imagine. Some people might even say that believing in yourself is borderline blasphemy. According to most viewpoints, we are supposed to believe in God's ability not ours. My answer to that is may surprise you.

God gave us the abilities we have. If you read Romans 12:3", something interesting is revealed. We are to think of ourselves according to the *"measure of faith"* God has allotted to us. As you read that verse in context with the surrounding verses you will notice something else. Paul is talking about having confidence in who we are in Christ. This is a term that I call Godfidence.

Hebrews 10:35 NKJV also tells us something of significance. *"Do not cast away your confidence which has great reward."* Confidence in the Bible is so important. In fact, you will find eighty-nine references to it in the Bible. You will find fifty-four of them occurring in the New Testament alone.

God has given us this; 'Godfidence' to be prepared for the task He has for us. If we didn't have the confidence that we could do something then it would be impossible for us to do it. What do I use as proof of this? Look at what Philippians 4:13 NLT says. *"For I can do everything with the help of Christ who gives me the strength I need."* So, based on this scripture, I am able to discover something important. I can walk in my Godfidence according to the ability Christ has given me.

In closing this chapter out, I would like for you to do one thing for me. You need to buy a journal, at the very least a notebook. I want you to start writing your feelings in it every day. It doesn't have to be a lot each day. It is only necessary that you write something each day. The reason for this is that I want you to start writing down your dreams and desires. I want you to be able to see if you are getting closer or further away from them.

One of my favorite verses in the Bible is found in Habakkuk 2:2-3 CEV; *"...I will give you my message in the form of a vision. Write it clearly enough to be read at a glance. At the time I have decided my words will come true. You can trust what I say about the future. It may take a long time, but keep on waiting—it will happen!"*

Don't give up! God is not done with you yet. He has a plan for you and He wants to make it plain for you to see. So write it down. That way when it does happen down the road, you can rejoice that God trusted you enough to show it to you. He did this even when you didn't fully understand what it meant. He did all this for you, because He loves you and has a plan for you. See you in the next chapter.

M.a.p. Your SOULUTION

Make a Plan
- Take a few minutes after reading this chapter and write down some notes about how you see yourself.
- How is this different than how you saw yourself before you started using drugs or alcohol? Please write that down as well. It is important to see these things in writing.

Accept Accountability {Recruit Partner(s) to Keep You Focused}
- For this MAP you will need to have an accountability partner that knew you before you got into your mess and one that knows you now that you are trying to change.
- Ask them if they wouldn't mind writing a one-paragraph statement about how they perceive you. What kind of person you are (kind, mean or indifferent).

Put it into Action
- Have everyone go out to coffee and look over the list. Now decide together, which is the one area that needs the most work.
- Next you will pick the opposite quality of what you all decide on. That week, you will make an effort to put forth that perception to everyone you come in contact with. This will begin to help you see yourself in a different perspective and hopefully uncover who you really are.

NOTES

NOTES

CONQUERING CHAOS

"For the Lord is God, and He created the heavens and earth and put everything in place. He made the world to be lived in, not to be a place of empty <u>chaos</u>... "
Isaiah 45:18 NLT

"The choice before us is plain: Christ or <u>chaos</u>, conviction or compromise, discipline or disintegration"
Rev. Peter Marshal,
Chaplain of the U.S. Senate in January 1947

CHAPTER 4
LOVE

Improve Your Identity

"If you don't know who you are, you'll end up as someone else."— Michael Dye[1]

Melody's struggles began at the age of nine when her parents got divorced. Her mom was dating a lot and wound up meeting someone on the Internet. She decided to move away and marry him. Neither Melody nor her brothers and sisters had any idea of what was going on.

After her mom left things were really hard. She struggled to fit in but never could. To make things worse she had no idea why she couldn't fit in. Even though she had friends, in her mind she would say things like, "These people don't like me. They think I'm weird. They think I'm different."

She didn't understand why she was like this all the time. She would get new friends only to push them away. She reasoned that she would rather be alone than have people in her life that could hurt her. She didn't realize this was a lie from the Devil that terrified her all the time.

For Melody, going to school every day was filled with anxiety. She wanted people to like her, yet at the same time she wanted to be alone so no one could hurt her. Her battle for acceptance continued all the way through middle school. It grew even worse in high school. Melody began to wonder if she would be able to have a normal conversation ever again. She wanted to connect with someone without wondering when the relationship would go bad.

Soon, she discovered that she could get attention from the boys in her High School. This opened up new doors for her. She liked the attention that she was getting. Then she would soon learn that they only wanted one thing. When she realized what they were after she just didn't care anymore. She decided that if that was the only way she was going to get acceptance and attention, then she would take it.

By the time she graduated High School she had already become an exotic dancer. This job finally allowed her to quit searching for acceptance. Here, people were paying money to spend time with her. To Melody it seemed as if people now wanted her acceptance. She liked it and got into it so much to where it didn't even faze her any more.

During this time in her life, she had pretty much fallen away from God. By the time she was eighteen she was living a very promiscuous lifestyle. This included alcohol, drugs, sex, and pretty much anything else.

She would use anything to cover up the hurt and pain of rejection she had dealt with pretty much her whole life. She had no idea who she was anymore. Her life was filled with worry, anxiety, and loneliness. She became more and more like the woman she portrayed at work and was a miserable person to be around.

A year later Melody remembers looking in the mirror and saying to herself, "Who am I?" She was no longer the person that she used to be. And she was nowhere near the person that she thought she would be by now. All she saw was darkness and confusion so she quit dancing.

She was now nineteen and was starting to lose everything. She lost her apartment, her car, and even her friends and family. She had also lost her identity and had no idea who she was anymore. She was doing a lot of drugs by now. She was using ecstasy, marijuana, or anything she could get a hold of. She wanted to take her mind off of the mess that she had gotten herself into.

In desperation Melody called out to her father for help. She told her dad that she needed his help because she didn't know who she was anymore. He told her that he couldn't help her because it was a spiritual battle. He said; "Satan wants to kill you but you belong to God. Do you remember when you gave your life to God?" She remembered the time when she asked God into her heart and the feeling she had. It was a feeling as if everything was brand new and she didn't have a care in the world. Her dad then continued; "God is calling you back to Him now. If you want the help you need then you need to find out who you are in Christ."

He asked her if she remembered their visit to California one summer. He was referring in particular about their visit to the Dream Center. In an ironic twist, Melody had been here to visit the Dream Center when she was thirteen. Her family had been giving donations to the Dream Center and wanted to see the place. So, they decided to take a vacation out there to see what it was all about. It seems that God had known who Melody was all along. He also knew the purpose He had for her life. He knew where she would be able to find her lost identity. It was time for her to start fulfilling the purpose He had designed for her before she was ever born.

Today Melody is living a life of hope and destiny. She now knows who she is but more importantly she knows to whom she belongs to. She is now a married woman. She desperately longs to see God do amazing things; in her life and; in the lives of her family and friends. She is using her rediscovered identity to help others. She has even gone back to the places she used to dance to give hope to those who feel just like she did a few years ago. She is a child of God.

Love Your Reflection

In this chapter we are going to explore several disciplines. These are disciplines that I believe make up the foundation of discovering your identity. Why is that important? We need to get to the place where we know who we are and what we are capable of. Once we find this out, then every life-controlling problem will begin to grow smaller. We must also learn to exercise our newfound faith in this new identity.

Since I am going to be talking about your identity, I need you to do something for me. I want you take a good, hard, look in the mirror. This is necessary if you want to learn your identity. How can you know who you are if you don't know what you look like?

It is also important if you want to break the oppression that has held you in bondage for so long. There are certain things you must learn to be on the lookout out for. This is critical if you want to be completely free of the chains that have formed in your life. In fact, I want to give you five reasons why it's time for you to do this in your life.

First and most importantly; you must be brutally honest with yourself. You cannot start your new life until you take a good, hard, and honest look at yourself. You need to see the self-imposed oppression and tyranny you are living under. Then, you must decide that it's time for you to fight back.

Next; you need to let someone else know about the way things are in your life. Since you are being honest with yourself this step is imperative that you follow through on. It's hard to come clean on something you have a tried to keep a secret for a very long time. You are afraid of what people will think or say about you. But, let me share something with you may not be aware of. Most of your friends already know that you have a problem.

The important thing here is to find somebody you know well enough that won't judge you for your past. But at the same time will be totally honest with you and keep you accountable in your new lifestyle. I know the question some of you are asking right now, "What if I mess up?" Well, let me put your fears to rest on this issue. You **will** mess up! That's why you need to be honest with yourself and tell someone else.

Next; you will need to overcome your fear of rejection. People will judge you and even reject you outright. It's a sad reflection on our society that this can and will happen most of the time.

It doesn't matter if people don't understand you. It is you who must come to an understanding. You are at war with an enemy that will stop at nothing until it has your life. It will have you doing things you never in a million years thought you would do.

You are not a failure for admitting that you want to change. In fact, the opposite is true. It takes courage to stand up to something that has had control of your life. It is time to be brave and say; "enough is enough?"

Another reason is that you will learn the true meaning of friendship. The truth of the matter is this. You may lose some friends in taking the steps that are being outlined here. But if that happens, ask yourself, if they were ever really your friends to begin with. True friends don't let their friends become trapped and do nothing about it.

Make no mistake about this choice. It will cost you, and sometimes, it will be severe. You may lose your job, your status in society, or sometimes even your church. Some people may even think of you as a bad person. But you must stand strong.

I've never been one to sugar coat things for people and I will not start here. You have to weigh the costs. You need to figure out what is the most important thing that needs to be done first. Then decide how much will it cost you? Only you can decide how much you're willing to put up with and if it is worth the rewards.

Finally; the one thing I can tell you is this. That eventually, the final reason will become clear to you. You will be able to walk in complete freedom and peace without the burden of your addictions. You can finally have a clear conscience in this area. You will know that you are on the right road. And most importantly, you will have help whenever you are in trouble and need it the most. In short, you will have soulutions for your problems. I am talking about problems that have been keeping you from becoming the person God intended you to become.

Love Your Faults

The next thing I need you to realize right now is this. You must focus on the harmful and negative side effects of your life-controlling problems. These have played out in your life like a bad dream. As you are thinking about those things I want you to take some time and write them down on a piece of paper. Use the example below that I have provided for you. So stop reading and do this exercise now.

Write the negative effect of your addiction below:	
My wife left me this morning. She said she was tired of all my excuses for coming home drunk.	
What was harmful about it?	*My relationship with my family has been destroyed.*
How did your actions affect you and the people around you?	*My wife will be a single mom and have to work to take care of the kids. My kids will not have a real relationship with me. It will be weekends only.*
What will be the benefits in your life if you quit your addictions?	*I will be able to be there for my children and my wife might want to come back to me.*

My hope is, that as you are doing this you will begin to see and understand the consequences of your negative actions. If you do, it will be somewhat easier to find your "reason why" for quitting. I say somewhat because this is based on logical thinking. And right now if you are in the middle of your addictions, let's face it. You are thinking anything but logically.

You may need a little help in this exercise. It's okay to have a trusted friend help you. I would even bet this is the same person that's always been there for you. But lately, even they don't come around as much, do they? Don't be tempted to give up at this point when you realize all the damage you may have caused. That is a normal response.

You wouldn't think of jumping from an airplane without a parachute, would you? It would most certainly end in tragedy and loss of life. If you can comprehend that last statement then there is some hope for you. You need to apply this same reasoning to your own life. Ask yourself this question. "Why do I keep using and abusing drugs and alcohol when I know it's causing me harm and problems in my own life even now?"

Let me ask you another question. What goes through your mind when you think about not being able to use or drink ever again? How does that make you feel? Don't just give an answer off the top of your head I want you to think long and hard about it.

If I were a gambling man, I would be willing to bet money that you have tried to quit before but something happened. Life became too full of stress without something to help you cope. You found it difficult to function without it. Maybe you just enjoyed the use of drugs and alcohol. More than likely, you most likely know what is needed in order for you to be free from the bondage of addiction. But for whatever reasons, you just can't seem do it. That, my friend, is the power of addiction.

It sneaks up on you and steals all your free will and power. You and I both know you may desperately want to stop this insanity called addictions. But part of you likes the feeling you get from using and partaking of the good times that come with the use of drugs.

All to well, *you* understand the negative feelings you encounter from using it. You know the shame that accompanies it. *You* definitely know the revolting and excruciating cost of what will happen if you keep using. And only *you* know, the unrestrained hostility and envy you feel towards others that are able to drink and use without consequences. *You* have asked yourself a million, make that a million and one times; "Why can't I be like them?"

But you fail to see the common factor in all these declarations is "*you*." If there is going to be a change then; guess what? *You* are going to have to something about it. *You* must first see that you are not a victim to this disorder. *You* must understand this one thing. There is a way to overcome the powerlessness of addictions and prevail against it.

You were created with a deep-seated belief in God of something greater than yourself. *You* are the only one that can turn your life over to that greater power that is God. Only then, can you receive a lasting soulution to your problem. And *you* are the one that must learn specific strategies to help you. You must train yourself to overcome these self-defeating prophecies in your life.

But this will only happen if *you* can see yourself as someone who is winning. You have to see yourself as someone who is already living a transformed, successful life. You have to come to the same conclusion that Melody did. That you are a child of God and He has something much, much better for you than the life you are now living.

Love Your Identity in Christ

Ever been asked the question, "Who are you?" Most of us probably have at one time or another. Stop and consider that question for a few seconds? I mean do we *really* know who we are? What is an identity?

The dictionary gives several meanings for identity[2]; 1) the condition of being oneself or itself, and not another, 2) the condition or character as to who a person or what a thing is, and 3) the sense of self, providing sameness and continuity in personality over time and sometimes disturbed in mental illnesses.

I don't know about you but when I look at those definitions I have a hard time believing them. I don't want to believe that who I am can be summed up in three textbook statements. I prefer to take the definition by June Hunt;

"The identity of a person is based on the distinguishing characteristics of that person. Your identity involves both your inner character and your outer conduct, which distinguishes you from everyone else. If you are a believer, your identity is grounded in who you are "in Christ." You have been born into a new family and given a new heart and have received the indwelling Holy Spirit. You have been set apart as a loved child of the living Lord and are being conformed to the very character of Christ."[3]

The concept of identity is far more than something lurking in our DNA. It is more than our life experiences. It is coupled with the foundation which was established in our childhood. And, if you are a child of God, it is even more. Your identity is wrapped up in the destiny God had chosen for you before you were even born. He loves you in spite of all the mess that you have gotten involved in. He wants to become your identity. We are a new person when we give our lives completely over to Him.

Discovering your identity is not an easy task. It involves an openness to face yourself in order to change. This is difficult because most people have been running from whom they are most of their life. But for true growth to take place you must move from beyond where you are, to where you want to be. To do this you requires you choose what is necessary. You have to develop a strategy of personal examination on a regular basis.

Searching yourself, routinely and persistently, allows you to discover flaws. You are able to see that you are falling way short of your potential identity. This is due in part, because you have lost your identity in Christ. Author Neil Anderson had this to say about discovering your God-given identity. *"...your hope for growth, meaning and fulfillment...is based on understanding who you are—specifically, your identity in Christ as a child of God."*[4]

So it stands to reason then, if we want to find out who we are then we must find our identity in Christ. Identity is way more than something you were born with. It is the way people perceive you; good or bad. And it is most likely based on your character, or lack of it, that determines this.

Love Your Character

As previously stated, most of us struggle with the concept of who we are. Some of us are confused because we literally don't know who one or both of our birth parents are. While this is becoming more and more common these days, it is still an important part of our identity. People will go their whole life thinking one thing about their family of origin. Then one day, they get hit with the phrase; "There's something we've been meaning to tell you." When you hear a statement like that, it is enough to question everything that you've ever been told.

Examples like the one above don't always have a happy ending. People get confused. They need some space, so they begin to isolate themselves. Unfortunately, it is from the individuals in their life that care about them the most. This sometimes leads people down a road of confusion and loneliness. When it gets to this point it sometimes seems as if there is only one option for them. A continual numbing of their constant, emotional pain can only satisfy this. The end result of all this is a life of bondage. This is what takes a person further and further away from the real individual they were created to be.

Character is more than just a word that makes a feeble attempt to explain your values. It is a lifestyle that tells the world who you are. You are either someone who can be trusted with a handshake. Or you are an individual that requires a thirty-seven-page contract, in triplicate, to be held to your word. The sad part of this comparison is that some of those individuals will even try to get out of a contract they created. They do this because something better has come along.

Struggling with your identity is an age-old problem that will be around for many more years to come. But I want you to understand this one thing. Your life was never created for you to live this way. When you look deep down inside your heart you know you were meant for something more than what you are doing now.

The behaviors you are allowing to take control of you now, is not who you are either. Most of you would've never believed me, or anybody else, if we had tried to tell you this before. You are flooded with unnatural desires. These desires have left you alone and fearful of what will happen next.

Your identity is also not wrapped up in your personality. Personality can change. But who you are at the core of your belief system is a constant that gives you balance in an ever-changing world. A great God, who has planned great things for your life, created you for greatness. The only person that can change that is you.

So what if things haven't gone according to your plan. It happens everyday to countless numbers of people. They don't throw in the towel on life and say it's not their fault. The victim card gets played way too much in our society. It's time for you to suck it up and meet life the way you were supposed to.

Besides, the excuses you are giving are bogus anyway. You and I both know that. You need to come to an understanding with yourself. Why? Because you are going to be around yourself for a very long time, so you might as well deal with the issues right now. "How do I do that?" you may be asking. We will talk about that in the next chapter.

Conclusion

What is it you dream about doing with your life? What is stopping you from doing just that? Most of the time, if we are honest with ourselves, it is because we don't see ourselves as that type of a person. But I want you to learn one thing from this chapter. It doesn't have to be a dream. It can be a new reality if you really want to take steps to make it happen.

Take a good hard look at yourself in the mirror and yourself some hard questions. What do you want out of life? What do you want to accomplish with the time you have on this earth? What type of a person do you want people to see you as. If you have come up with some answers to those questions, then you have a good picture or reflection of what you want to see when you look in the mirror.

In closing, I want you to promise me one thing. Don't focus on your faults other than to identify them and what caused them to manifest in your life. Once you have done that, you have armed yourself with the necessary tools. It is now time to start eradicating them one by one. Then start replacing them with the answers to the questions you find in the Word of God. This is really the key to improving your identity.

One of the most important ways to continue improving your identity is this. You must make sure you are standing firm in your identity as a believer of Christ. If you don't know who you are in

Him, you will search and search and search but never find out who you are. He is the beginning place for everything. We cannot be who we dream to be without having a foundation in His Word. His Word is life and it gives us life and makes us identify with Him as heirs to a universe given to us by God.

When you have done all the above, then you are ready to reveal the true character of who God created you to be. You are more than what you see in the mirror. You are your actions, beliefs and thoughts based upon your core belief system. Don't settle for less than who God created you to be. Rise up and be the man or woman of God who is planted deep in His Word. Be someone who has the very character of God coursing through your veins.

Then, and only then, are you ready to embrace your identity in Christ. This is an identity that was paid for by the blood of Jesus Christ. He is the one and only Son of God. Once you have done this, you can then eradicate the false image created by evil desires.

FOOTNOTES

[1] The Genesis Process for Change Groups, Book 2, Individual Workbook, Dye, Michael, (Self Published, 2006), page 25.

[2] **American Psychological Association (APA):** identity. (n.d.). *Dictionary.com Unabridged (v 1.1)*. Retrieved September 01, 2008, from Dictionary.com website: http://dictionary.reference.com/browse/identity

Chicago Manual Style (CMS): identity. Dictionary.com. *Dictionary.com Unabridged (v 1.1)*. Random House, Inc. http://dictionary.reference.com/browse/identity (accessed: September 01, 2008).

Modern Language Association (MLA): "identity." *Dictionary.com Unabridged (v 1.1)*. Random House, Inc. 01 Sep. 2008. <Dictionary.com http://dictionary.reference.com/browse/identity>.

[3] "Identity." *Hope For The Heart Biblical Keys Glossary* © 2005 by *Hope For The Heart*. Hunt, June

[4] Victory Over the Darkness. Anderson, Neil T. (Ventura, CA: Regal Books, 2000), page 24

M.A.P. Your SOULUTION

Make a Plan
- On a separate piece of paper or in your journal, write down the first three words that describe you and your character.
- Next, write down what you would like your character to be. In other words, what kind of person would you like to be known as?

Accept Accountability {Recruit Partner(s) to Keep You Focused}
- Next, interview three of your friends and ask them the same thing.
- Once you get all the answers back compare them and look for common answers. This will give you a good start to determine your true identity.
- Share with this friends you answers above and ask them to keep you accountable in becoming the person you want to be.

Put it into Action
- Take out your list of what you want to be known as or your new identity and look it over, meditating on what types of actions are required from you to be this person.
- Next, find opportunities to exercise these actions in your everyday life. Don't just dream about doing it, actually find ways you can make this part of your identity today.

NOTES

NOTES

CHAPTER 5

UNLEASH

Release Your Revolution

"No big revolution is possible without small personal revolution, on a personal level. It must first happen inside."
- Jim Morrison[1]

Miguel grew up in the urban gang culture of East Los Angeles. He was a typical teenager from the barrio. As a result of his surroundings and influence from some of his family members, he eventually wound up in a gang. The years that followed were filled with drugs, drinking and despair. He had been sucked into a world of violence where "kill or be killed" was a way of life. One night while he was home sleeping, the S.W.A.T. team came and arrested him for murder.

The days and months that followed became a nightmare for his mother as she prayed for his soul. While he was awaiting his trial, locked up in the LA County Jail, someone gave him a Bible. He didn't know much about it. He had been raised Catholic and only went to church every once in awhile. One night after reading it, he cried out to God and asked Him to help him get out of the mess he was in.

The day of his trial came. The evidence was presented, and after a lengthy court process, he was released. All charges against him had been dropped. While Miguel was in jail, he had heard about the Dream Center. He wanted to honor God for what He had done for him. So, at the urging of his mother he decided to come into our program.

I would love to say everything went according to his plan. But that is not usually the way life works out. He was still full of violence and hate for everyone, including himself. I even have a picture that shows just how hard he was. We were on a beach trip with everyone in the program one day. We would do this sometimes during the summer to get them off campus so they could unwind and blow off some steam. We also would have a baptism for those wanting to be baptized.

As I was explaining the purpose of baptism, someone took a picture of us. And off to the side was Miguel. He was "mean-mugging" me trying to intimidate me and to see if I was for real. Miguel would later explain to me that he was just checking me out to see if what I was saying was for real or if it was all an act.

I would constantly be making statements about how much I loved the people under my care. I talked about how glad I was that God had given me the opportunity to be able to show them the love of a father. So Miguel had decided to test me and see if my love was real or not. Although Miguel and I never had any physical confrontations, he did watch my life. It was not an easy process for him to learn to trust people. Especially to individuals who were former, rival gang members. He had a street and prison mentality and it showed up in his personality and actions. But little by little his stone cold heart was turning into a heart of flesh.

As Miguel neared his one-year anniversary of coming into the program he came to talk to me. He was looking forward to his graduation date and he had decided what he wanted to do. I remember looking at him as a proud Papa looks at his son. He had changed so much. He was so excited he could hardly wait to tell me, just like a little kid.

He was going to stay on as a second year volunteer so he could get his G.E.D. From there he wanted to go on and become a drug and alcohol counselor. When I asked him why he wanted to do this he just grinned and said that he was so thankful for this place. He believed that since we had taken care of him for one year, he wanted to give back to others. He hoped that maybe he could help someone else that was just like him.

His life had truly been turned around. He was now living a life of integrity, honor and character. His mother and other family members had also noticed the change in him. He was not the same person as when he came into the program. He was a completely new creation, just like the Bible says in 1 Corinthians 5:17. The old gang member from East Los Angeles was gone and the new and improved version had just been released.

The journey for Miguel is not over. In fact, it is just beginning. Miguel received his G.E.D. Soon after that, he started his classes to become a certified drug and alcohol counselor. Don't get me wrong; Miguel is not perfect in his walk. He still battles his demons but he is continuing the revolution he started towards a new life.

Unleash Your Motivation

Revolution is defined as a forcible overthrow of government or social order in favor of a new system. Some of its synonyms include; rebellion, revolt, insurrection, etc. The word "revolution" comes from the Latin word *revolutio*. This means a "turn around" or a fundamental change in power or organizational structure that takes place in a relatively short period of time.

The American Revolution is an example of this type of revolution. The existing government was overthrown in favor of a new form of self-government. This new form of government became known as a democracy. And with that the United States of America was born.

Likewise, if you want a new form of government in your life you need to have your own personal revolution. In order to do this, you have to turn your life around. You do this by changing the power that controls how you live your life and make choices. In other words, you must start a revolution in your life.

In the grand scheme of things, you must make that decision in a relatively short period of time. If you delay this processes in your life, studies have shown that more than likely you will never start. You can't just sit around and contemplate things forever. You have to eventually do what the American colonists did. You must fight for your new way of life and overthrow the old way. This includes, anything and anyone that would prevent your freedom from becoming a reality.

In the early days of the American Revolution they would send riders across the country with a call to arms. This was their way of letting people know there was a battle coming and they needed to prepare for it. You are in for the battle of your life and you need to prepare for it. You must have your own call to arms. Tell everyone you know what you are facing and that you need all the help you can get to fight this battle.

I know there may be some of you that feel something rising up within you right now. You are ready to go forth and conquer. But I need to give you a reality check. Real life is not like the movies. Everything doesn't always turn out so pretty in the end.

There will be casualties along the way. This can appear in the form of lost relationships with friends and family members. In reality, it can be anyone who is unprepared for the new you. You have to count the cost and be ready to make sacrifices in order to win the freedom you deserve.

Unleash Your Understanding

Continuing to be successful to the resistance of your self-defeating actions can be difficult. It is a sometimes painful and trying process. It's not easy to change your frame of mind on whom you are supposed to become overnight. Change is a process and it takes time. Sometimes it passes quickly and at other times, well; let's just say a turtle can run faster.

To make this change lasting, you have to see yourself in a different way. You have to have a vision of who you were meant to be and be willing to fight for that vision, to the death if necessary. Look at the example of the American Revolution. The Colonists may have declared their independence in 1776 with the Declaration of Independence. However, they didn't receive the full victory until 1783, after many years of fighting.

To understand this revolution, we have to understand the enemy. So then, let's look at our enemy from a medical perspective.

Most drugs are formulated to help us overcome medical discomfort. They may enable your body to fix or repair itself. Some are designed to ease pain. Some will help you to rest. They may keep you from becoming angry. They may help you overcome feelings of anxiety, and hopelessness. Others drugs are able to help you handle stress. Still others can arouse sexual excitement. And, there are those that are created to help you drop your weight.

Drugs, in general, have an effect on us in many ways. Our society, for the most part, views drugs as the answer to all our problems. With this mindset it is easy to believe that they can cure us from whatever may be troubling us.

But let's think about that statement for a minute. If that were true, wouldn't the world have been cured of all its evils a long time ago? And why is it that every new pill is advertised as being the next "wonder drug". In fact, it's probable that you started using drugs that were prescribed by a doctor.

Or, it may have been because you wanted to fit in with your friends. Why not? It seemed like everybody else around you was using them. So that made it even easier for you to start using them as well. Obviously, this is where things get a little messy.

People become addicted to substances not because they're bad for you. They like having that feeling of euphoria from using drugs. It becomes a problem when you have to have it in order to cope with everyday living. It becomes a problem, when feel you can't make it through the day on your own. You feel as though you need to use some substance, to ease the discomfort of reality.

This is how addictions are formed. But then again, you're a smart person and you already knew that. You're not going to let yourself get to the point of using drugs to escape life's everyday problems, are you? You know how easy it is to become addicted before you even know what's happening. So you're good here? Right? No problems or denial going on here, right? So if you're good with this, then I urge you to keep on reading, if you dare!

The medical research field has shown us there are two major

causes of physical addiction. The first one is that your cells adapt to the substances that are introduced into your body on a regular basis. The second one is that your metabolism will become more efficient at processing drugs. Your organs become able to break down the toxins faster from these substances you put into your body. In other words, the stuff you are putting into your body becomes a normal happening for your cells. They can even get to a point to where they come to expect it on a regular basis.

Whenever you put these substances, or toxins in your body, something happens internally. Your blood will take it to every living cell. You become tolerant to drugs when your cells have learned to overcome their effects on the body. Essentially, they have become trained to protect themselves against the poison in the drugs. In order to do this, the cell walls become toughened. This is how they maintain their strength and diminish the harmful effect these toxins have on you.

But, there is something even more sinister at work here. As your cells get tougher, it takes more of the drug to produce the effect or "high" that you feel. That's the main reason for taking the drug in the first place. As a result of this, you are able to consume more and more drugs as your cells get used to it. But even, the cell walls give in and break down. And sometimes-irreversible damage is done.

When you have reached this stage it becomes dangerous and threatening to your body. Your cells have lost their capacity to keep the poisons out. Thus, they are no longer able to receive nutrients necessary for the survival of the cell. At this point a lot of them will stop working or begin to operate in an irregular way. This is also why people tend to look all sucked-up, like a walking skeleton. They have lost their desire for anything but their drugs. This is when your major organs such as the heart, brain, liver, or lungs start to shut down.

Metabolism also has a part to play in this tragedy called addiction. It is very closely associated with what you eat. Your body will metabolize or break down the food you eat into its basic building blocks of life. These include such things as vitamins, minerals, amino acids, etc. This is done in order to get these critical elements to the cells so they can be used.

The reason all this happens is to make use of anything that you put into your body. This is how the body is able to grow and function on a variety of different diets. Your body has been made to gain sustenance from anything you put into it. You truly are what you eat.

Your metabolism also helps in this process. It works by getting rid of poisonous and toxic substances that get introduced into the body. The liver is the organ that plays the main role in this course of action. The liver will look at these substances as unwanted chemicals. It will then start creating enzymes to neutralize these toxins.

If you continue using a particular substance on a consistent basis something amazing happens. Your liver will get better at removing it from your system. It's almost as if your liver will come to "anticipate" that particular substance. It will produce enzymes that are ready and waiting for the substance.

This is another key reason that tolerance increases. That is why it takes greater and greater doses of a drug to get the same original effects. This is also a reason why people tend to feel pain during withdrawals. Your liver has come to anticipate your addiction. It will have all these counter-toxins ready to go. But, there is nothing to neutralize so the body reacts in a negative way to the lack of the substance.

To provide a counter offensive to this attack, you will have to be in rebellion against your senses. Every sense inside of you is telling you that you need this substance to survive. But, this is a lie that will keep you locked in your hellish nightmare forever. Only you can decide if you have had enough. Are you ready to fight to regain your freedom?

Unleash Your Transformation

Okay, now I want you to stop, take some time to be honest with yourself. Think about this next statement. If you keep on doing the same old thing, you'll keep on getting the same frustrating results. You need to take a good, hard look at the person staring back at you in the mirror. Look at the person you've become. You're jacked up. You've got bloodshot eyes, your house is a wreck, and you haven't visited your family in months.

In fact, you've been avoiding all the people who care about you. All they want to talk about is how bad you need help. Let's face reality here. It's time to check yourself and see what the problem is. Stop reading this for a minute and go to the nearest mirror. I want you to take a good hard look and ask yourself the following question;

"Are there times in my life when I sometimes wonder if I really do have a problem?" If you have a hard time answering that question, or if the answer is yes, then you may have a problem with addictions or other life-controlling problems. If you did answer yes then you are ready to continue reading. If you answered no, then you obviously don't have a problem and this book is not for you. But, maybe you know someone that can benefit from this book, so you might want to keep reading anyway.

So much of the time, people that are using drugs will deny they have a problem. Even worse, they will hide it from everyone, including himself or herself, by making excuses. Why is this? It's only natural for you to defend yourself. Especially if it is in the form of accusations that could be damaging to your well-being, as you perceive it.

But every so often these defenses will break down and cause you to reflect on what is going on in your life. It is during this time of reflection you think that just maybe, you might have an ever so slight problem. So, if you think you might have some struggles in this area of your life, chances are you probably do.

I want you to reflect for just a minute with me if you will. How do you feel the morning after you have used some sort of

116

substance? You may have used to feel better about yourself, cope with life or just unwind with some friends.

Are you in pain all over your body? Is your head foggy? Do you feel embarrassed for giving in to temptation to use? Did you promise yourself that this is the last time you will feel this way ever again? Did you make a decision that you are going to quit using and throw all your drugs away as soon as you feel better?

Are you angry with yourself? Do you feel sorry for yourself and want to do something that will help you change your ways? Do you give in to your own thoughts for recovery after you use and your defense mechanisms are down?

But then, you start feeling better and the day marches on. You begin to get a little clearer in your thinking. Your defenses soon come back on-line. At this point, you may begin to make excuses for yesterday's minor indiscretion. You may even justify what happened with excuses. "*I had a bad day*". "*I didn't have enough to eat*". "*I had a really stressful day with the boss*". Or, it could be some other excuse that doesn't make much sense to anyone but you.

Life goes on and you will give in to the temptation to use or drink again. "*Just a little bit to take the edge off,*" is what you say. You are trying to convince yourself that it's okay to use again. Yesterday was different and after all, you're off work today so it won't be the same. But the vicious cycle continues.

If you're reading this and it hits home with you then you have got to answer this question. What are you thinking? Why would you want to keep on doing something that makes you suffer in such a terrible way? Why does your body crave something that has so many bad consequences for you? Things will never change until you decide that it's time for a change.

Unleash Your Power

There is an old song by Steve Camp that has become my anthem over the years. It has been a guiding light to help me see the real reason Christ came to this earth to do. He came to help restore us to a right, **real**-ationship with God. The words to the first verse follow...

Some people want to live,
Within the sound of chapel bells,
But I want to run a mission,
A yard from the gates of hell,
And with everyone you meet,
Take them the gospel and share it well,
Look around you as you hesitate,
For another soul just fell,
Let's run to the battle[2]

In February of 2003, that song became more than an anthem to me. It became a way of life. In December, of the previous year, my mentor and I had been talking about my future. He was also a long-time friend, so he didn't pull any punches. He asked me if I had ever thought of going to the Dream Center.

Little did I know than in three short months I would be living and ministering in that very place. This was a place, where God had allowed my passion and purpose to collide. In my wildest dreams, I never would have imagined being in a place as fantastic as the Dream Center. I was going to be working with my heroes of the faith. These were none other than Pastors Tommy & Mathew Barnett.

As I am telling this story to you, I know some of you may be asking; "Why is this story important?" It is important because it's not just about me. It is also about you and others like you that are struggling with life-stuff. I learned a valuable lesson in all the stuff that happened to me. It doesn't matter where you came from. It only matters where you're going.

God wants to be God of your stuff. However ugly or beautiful it is. That may not seem like a very theological principle to you, but if you stop and think about it, it really is true. Let me tell you why. Because if He is God of your stuff, then He is God of you, and everything you do.

God has taken this washed up, twice-divorced preacher, and transformed me. I am now an instrument of change for thousands of people over the last decade. I am living on "Fantasy Island" every day I wake up. I get to do something I enjoy. Encouraging people to see themselves as God sees them. It doesn't matter how many times you have tried to get your life back on track. It only matters that you try one more time.

Having a child of my own has given me a natural father's heart. But God has magnified that many times over. He has allowed me to show many individuals what the love of a father is all about. I am getting to show them about the love of THE Father. And in doing so, they are able to experience a love that transcends all of time and circumstance.

Maybe you are struggling right now with that concept. Your idea of a father is just someone who donated sperm to your mother in order to give you life. If you truly want to change the way you are then you must start a revolution in your own life. You must see God as the loving father you never had.

In the American Revolution, the colonists had reached a turning point in their history. They were being forced to give support to a government, which they had no say. So, they started their revolution with an act of sacrifice. They destroyed something they thought they could not live without. They dumped their tea into the ocean in response to illegal taxation. That act of sacrifice became the passion to fuel their power. They used that to overthrow their oppressors.

If you are ready to create your own revolution, you must also follow their example. Are you willing to throw away whatever is keeping you from exercising your freedom? It's time to get plugged into a power that can help you conquer the chaos that has you in bondage. It's time to choose your side now!

Conclusion

Revolution is such a powerful concept. It is the idea that has fueled passions since the beginning of time. At its core is a belief that there is something better out there for you. But it doesn't come easy. It always requires a price. Miguel had come to a place where he was ready to sacrifice his old life to have his own personal revolution. The question you have to ask yourself is; "Am

I at that place yet?"

Sometimes you realize you can't do it alone and you need help. Any kind of help will do when you are in that desperate of a place. But it takes motivation, inspiration, and a passion to see the process through. While you may be weak, there are lots of people who will come to your rescue. They are ready to help you fight this, if you will just issue your own call to arms. But, a lot of times, we find ourselves facing incredible odds that overwhelm us. However, just knowing we have someone by our side, helping us fight, gives us the ability to believe we can win.

Don't ever underestimate your enemy. Know what you are up against. Know your own weaknesses as well. That is the only way you can hope to win. Just as our bodies are designed to help heal us, so too, are our souls.

Eternity was created in us when God breathed into us and we became a living soul. Freedom, however, is not realized until we accept one important fact. It is only through God that we can have freedom from bondage throughout all eternity.

This is how true transformation comes about. By coming to a place in our lives where we realize that, in order to change, we must embrace eternity with God. If we truly are honest with ourselves, we will learn a life-changing truth. That is, eternity without God is nothing short of hell. I think most of us have had our fill of what hell has offered us so far. Don't you?

So be honest with yourself for once! What is it that you are afraid of? You have nothing to fear. In fact, **F.E.A.R.** is nothing but a **F**alse **E**xpectations **A**bout **R**eality. When you realize that God has given you power over all the power of the enemy, you are invincible. This same **F.E.A.R.** will then turn into a battle cry to **F**ace **E**verything **A**nd **R**ise! So what are you waiting for? Start your own call to arms by calling someone right now and tell them you are ready to start your own revolution.

FOOTNOTES

[1] Morrison, J. (n.d.). Search results for: revolution. . Retrieved July 15, 2014, from http://statusmind.com/page/2/?s=revolution

[2] *Run to the Battle*, Lyrics by Steve Camp © Warner/Chappell Music, Inc.

M.A.P. Your SOULUTION

Make a Plan
- Take some time to meditate and then write down the things in your life that you need to unleash your revolution on.
- Write down what sacrifices you are willing to make in order to realize your own revolution?

Accept Accountability {Recruit Partner(s) to Keep You Focused}
- Have an accountability partner write down a list of self-destructive things they know about you that you need to revolt against.
- Make a list of individuals you know that would answer a call to arms to come to your aid.

Put it into Action
- Using the list above – write out steps for each item that you can take right now to unleashing your freedom.
- Make this list with four columns; the first column with the description of what you need to do, the second column with the steps you need to take to make it happen, the third column with the people who are going to help you, and the fourth column for the date you complete it.

NOTES

NOTES

CHAPTER 6

TARGET

Launch Your Legacy

*"The choices we make about the lives we live
determine the kind of legacies we leave."*
— *Tavis Smiley*[1]

In my time ministering to people who struggle with authority issues, I have learned a few things. One of those being that it's not usually the loud obnoxious people that cause the most trouble. In fact, it is usually the opposite. The quiet ones are the ones that you have to watch out for. Eddie was one of the quiet ones that came into the program in my early years at the Dream Center.

Eddie's mother had died when he was only eleven years old. This left a huge void in his life during his adolescent years. It is during this time of life, when boys are turning into young men. This is crucial age for a young boy. He needs to have a mother's love shaping his life. It is helpful in smoothing out the rough edges of a young life. Eddie was robbed of that and as a result, he lost himself. The only way he knew how to cope was by using drugs.

Eddie also became infatuated with the hip-hop culture during this time. This led him to a church that ministered to youth using this as a vehicle. At the age of thirteen he gave his life over to Jesus, but his struggles were far from over. He still struggled with drugs and was in and out of trouble. They had such a stronghold on his life that he continued to get worse. He continued that way until 2004, when his pastor finally sent him to us to see if we could help him.

Eddie had reached a point in his life where he was ready for change. He was nearly twenty-one now and saw no future for himself in his present state. After all, he had been using drugs now for over ten years and he was ready for a change. He embraced what the program had to offer him and before long completed it. He chose to stay a second year to prepare himself even more.

Eventually he got involved in a ministry that toured around the world. They used hip-hop as a tool to help troubled youths turn their lives around. Today he is married to a lovely, God-fearing wife and has two beautiful kids. He has helped to plant a church that ministers to the hip-hop culture. He has even started his own ministry to continue to reach out to those of that genre. He truly is creating a legacy that will outlast him.

But it didn't come easy. He had to work on his relationship with God and on his skills to be successful in creating a legacy that would last. But one of the greatest things he learned was to believe in himself and in the abilities God had given him.

Launch Into Your Destiny

Previously, we briefly discussed about God's purpose for your life. I want to continue that discussion here in this section with more depth. But before I do that I must first ask you the question, "What is destiny?" Have you ever wondered what your destiny is? All of us probably do at one time or another. The dictionary defines destiny as one of the following;

- *The inevitable or necessary fate to which a particular person or thing is destined; one's lot.*
- *A predetermined course of events considered as something beyond human power or control.*
- *The power or agency thought to predetermine events.*[2]

The general concept given here is that destiny is something that we are not in control of. It is something beyond us. Perhaps something that was even put into motion long before we ever walked upon this earth. Whatever the case may be the meaning is clear; that is, your path has already been laid out for you to walk on.

Having said that, I do need to make some clarification here. Just because a path or destiny has been laid out for you, doesn't mean that is where you will end up. In fact, for most of us, that is far from the reality that we have found ourselves in.

The reason for the difference in what we were destined to do versus where we settled boils down to just on word. It is simply choice. You have been created for a specific destiny, or place in God's purpose. Yet, you still have free will to make your own choices. And sadly, most of us choose a destiny other than what we were created for.

I have never met anyone who thought; "I wonder how much I can mess up my destiny today by the bad choices I will make." Usually, it is because we are caught up with something or someone. We will align ourselves with something we shouldn't be associating with. This in turn, leads us down a road of bad choices. And it is because of these bad choices that will lead to a lost legacy. Good or bad, we are defined by our past choices.

But you don't have to be in despair over this. Pastor Matthew preached a sermon one time that radically changed my life. I developed a new perspective at the way I look at ministry in general. It is brilliant in its simplicity. It is about, at its core, creating a new legacy. Here is the truth that blew me away; "You can change your past!" At first, I thought he didn't know what he was talking about but then he went on to explain it this way. "If you change what you do right now it will change your past. Because what you do now will become yesterday, and yesterday is in the past.

So, what you do today becomes your past tomorrow." This will also change your legacy because your legacy is defined by what you leave behind. Destiny is not so much about your destination as it is about your journey to arrive there. It is a road that we travel upon that will lead us to our final destination. Therefore, whatever you do today will change your legacy for the future. And you do it by changing your past. I know. Don't think about too hard. It gave me a headache. But, it works.

Launch Into Your Journey

The scripture does tend to agree with this same general concept. It does so by describing destiny as a road that is traveled upon. But it does give us just a little more insight. It is not described as mere chance that just happens, or even fate, in which we have no choice. But it is something much, much more than that.

For example take a look at the word, *fate* in Ecclesiastes 9:2 NASB. The original word here means chance happening. But the root here is from a word that is similar to *floor* or *roof*. But, the meaning is more than just a roof you happen be under or floor you happen to run across.

It is more like this. The roof or floor was laid out for a specific purpose. Meaning it was built with a design for everything to be in its proper place. If one board is out of place then there is the risk of falling through. The meaning is clear. It means that even though you may happen to walk across this floor or be under this roof, it was designed to help you.

It may have been an accident that you walked across the floor. But it is no accident in what the floor was designed to do for you. The same is true for the roof. It may be accidental that you took shelter under it. But it was no accident in what the roof was designed for. It was crafted to keep out and protect you from whatever harmful elements are outside.

Whether it is a roof or a floor they both have one thing in common. There has to be a foundation it is built upon. So it is the same with our destiny. There must be a foundation that holds up the floor we walk on that leads to our destiny. It is imperative in order for us to be sure we are on the right path to our destiny. The foundation is also important to hold up the roof. It is the roof that will protect us from the harmful elements that would delay our journey.

You're chomping at the bit right now to ask aren't you? What is that foundation? It is quite simply that God loves you and wants to have fellowship with you. He wants to be there with you as you walk on the road to your destiny He has created just for you. And guess what? It's not a secret that He is trying to keep from you. He wants you to know and understand the purpose that He has for your life. It is one that He has laid out for you from the very beginning, even before you were born. In fact, it has been the same for everyone. Ever since Adam fell out of intimate fellowship with God, He has been building a foundation for us. This foundation is designed to reestablish an intimate relationship with us.

The key to understanding this is found in Romans 8:28 NLT. *"And we know that God causes everything to work together for the good of those who love God and are called according to his purpose for them."* We may not always understand the reason why God has placed us where we are. But we can have confidence in knowing that His plan is perfect and it will work out for our good in the end.

I think maybe sometimes it's easy to confuse the reason for wanting to change. We think that our behavior and destiny are intertwined. But, the reality here is that they are two different things. Our destiny is who God created us to be. Our behavior is based upon our circumstances or whatever we are feeling at the time. I know that was a mind-blowing moment for some of you, just like it was for me. It was almost as if a light bulb switched on over your head just now. I can even hear some of you screaming; "That's it, that's what it is!"

It's normal to struggle with the big question as to why we are here. We all do from time to time. The big question here is not why, but how. "How do I discover my destiny?" Let me answer this by saying, it's really not as difficult as people make it out to be. Some people want to make it out to be some great mystery that will one day be revealed to you when you get to heaven. You imagine this happening in the midst of some great *aha* moment where you get struck by a bolt of revelation lightning. When in reality, it's been right in front of us all along. I have learned to break it down into the following seven words; *see, sense, suppose, shift, speak, show* and *share*. How can it be that simple? Let me **show** you.

First, you must **see** what's in your hand. God has given you a specific set of gifts and talents. He gave those to you with a specific purpose in mind. That purpose is to be able to find your place in His grand purpose or plan. Some people call it the *calling of God*. This calling is not to be confused with a calling into full-time ministry. It is your vocational calling. It is something that is easy for you to do and that you enjoy doing.

Second, you must **sense** or feel what is in your heart. What is in your heart is your passion. It is a burning desire that consumes your thoughts on a constant basis. It is what you dream of doing. It is what you would be doing if time or money were no boundary for you. It is something you would do you even if you didn't get paid for doing it.

Third, you need to **suppose** or have a vision of what's in your hand and what's in your heart working together. This is God's ultimate plan for you. But it may take some time for the two to come together. This is where you learn the true meaning of patience. You must work faithfully with what is in your hand until you are able to merge it with what is in your heart.

Fourth, you must **shift** your thoughts. This is necessary in order to kill the Automatic Negative Thoughts or A.N.T.s[3] as I like to call them. Your thoughts are very powerful and they will set the course for your destiny. You must stomp on all of the A.N.T.'s in your life. What are those? They are those thoughts that just pop into your mind automatically. They are the ones that yell and scream at you when you are staring at yourself in the mirror.

They may be thoughts such as the following. *"You're ugly!" "You'll never amount to anything." "Why am I so stupid?"* These thoughts are very dangerous and will steer you off course if you let them. They cannot be allowed to dominate your mind. You must take Philippians 4:8 NIV as your motto. *"Finally, brothers, whatever is true, whatever is noble, whatever is right, whatever is pure, whatever is lovely, whatever is admirable — if anything is excellent or praiseworthy — **think** about such things."*

Fifth, you must **speak** words of life and not death. Proverbs

18:20-21, TEV says this. "*You will have to live with the consequences of everything you **say**. What you **say** can preserve life or destroy it; so you must accept the consequences of your **words**.*" If you say you are an addict, then you will be an addict. If you say you are a person delivered from the bondage of addictions, then you are delivered.

Sixth, you must **show** what it is you are doing. There is a time for talking and planning and there is a time for doing. When it is all said, then it eventually has to be done. There is an old saying from John Maxwell that goes like this. "*People don't care how much you know until they know how much you* care."[4] People need to see you walking in your destiny. It is not enough just to talk about doing it. You must do it!

Seventh and finally, you must **share** what God has done for you. It doesn't do anybody any good if they never find out about the miracles that God has done in your life. The concept of sharing your testimony to help others has been around for ages. And, in every situation where it has been used, victories have occurred. It brings healing to the person sharing and hope to the one's that are listening. Don't underestimate the power of your story. It has been said that you can't have a testimony without a test or a message without a mess.[5]

These are the basics of what you need to know to start learning about your destiny. Before I understood this concept, it was hit or miss for me. I just always figured that my revelation would come to me like a lightning bolt out of the sky. But, I finally figured out that's not how it's done. The Bible, in fact, tells us that God uses the simple things to confuse the wise. God made things really simple for us. We are the ones who make things complicated.

Launch Into the Supernatural

When you think about your destiny sometimes it can be overwhelming. Did you ever stop to ponder why that is? It is because destiny is beyond our own abilities. It takes something more that what we have to make it happen. If you don't believe this then take a look at all the examples in the Bible. Pay particularly close attention to those in the book of Hebrews chapter eleven.

This passage of scripture is known as the Hebrews Hall of Faith. It is called that because it talks about the faith of those that did great things for God. There is one interesting thing about all these people. Their lives were pretty jacked up before they discovered their destiny. But that's not the most amazing part of it all. They couldn't walk in their destiny while they were still messed up. That's why something supernatural had to happen in their lives.

But, get this; the supernatural occurrence wasn't just for the event. It was also for them. They needed to experience the supernatural in their lives on their own. They needed this in order to be transformed from the ordinary to the extraordinary. They needed to experience the supernatural transforming power of God first. Why? It was because they knew their own weaknesses. They knew it was so big; they couldn't do it on their own. They needed God.

Can you imagine the irony of it all? That the God of the universe would choose somebody unqualified, over someone qualified. He needed somebody ordinary to perform something outrageous. That was the only way that you knew it had to be God, in order for that person to pull it off? That is the miracle space. It is that area just out of reach of your abilities and limitations. That is the area God likes to work in. It is the area where the natural becomes super so that supernatural miracles can take place.

The miracle is not that God reveals to us what our purpose is in life. The miracle is that He has designed us for something that is far beyond our own ability to accomplish on our own. He looks at our life that is jacked up, tore up, and beat up and says, "*That one, I can use him. He's so messed up everyone will know it's me and not him that is making miracles happen.*"

I know this can be pretty confusing at times. We know who we are, so when we see something miraculous happen with us at the center of it we are in shock. We ask ourselves; "How can God use someone like me?" And if you're like me, you probably don't know what you're doing half the time, anyway. So how can you help anybody? You need to help yourself first!

Our destiny has been laid out before us like a road but it's not set in stone. It's dependent on our choices, so it can be changed, for good or for bad. It is something so great that we can't even begin to understand why God would ever do such a thing for us. Just look at what Paul says in Ephesians 3:20; "*Now to him who is able to do far more abundantly beyond all that we ask or think, according to the power that works in us*". The miracle is not in the destiny. The miracle is in the fact that you are even on the journey at all!

God can give you a new destiny in a heartbeat. The miracle is in us doing it. It is in us becoming the miracle...to our family, our friends, people that will cross our path. All for the reason to show the world that He is God and He wants a relationship with us no matter how bad our life is messed up.

Because when you discover your destiny you will discover the miracle that God created you to be. That, my friend, is life changing. For in that miracle is the power of your recovery. You are no longer walking around trying to figure out who you are. Destiny requires miracles but many times it requires you to BE the miracle.

Launch Into Your Focus

I know this is a lot to take in right now but I need your undivided attention for a few moments more. Understanding your destiny is difficult to begin with. And, if you add, believing in the miracle that God has created you to be, that makes it even more difficult. All this together can be an overwhelming thought to process. But there is more to walking in your recovery than just that.

Some of you just sat upright in your chair and said; "I knew it! Here's the disclaimer, right?" No, there's no disclaimer. It is simply a continuation of the process of walking in your destiny. Remember that I already mentioned destiny is like a road that has been built for you. You have been shown which way to go but it is up to you to choose whether or not you go that way.

This is the area that causes a lot of people to fail. They will

133

receive a revelation about their destiny. Then, while they are walking on that road, they begin to get distracted by the things that are on the side of the road. And, somewhere down the road, the temptation gets too much to handle. They mess up and fall by the side of the road.

This happens because mainly as the result of one thing. They have been looking at the distractions on the side of the road. They let their focus drift in what the Bible calls "vain imaginations". So, instead of walking in their destiny, they forget the reason they have been placed on the road. And that is to help others along the way make it to their destination. So, eventually they stray off the road and give into temptation.

Does this mean they weren't walking in their destiny, NO! What it means is that they stopped paying attention to their destination. They also will fail in the little details that God had given them to do. It is important to pay attention to these as these help to keep you on track.

It's kind of like having a car. You can get a brand new car and enjoy driving in it so much that you just keep driving. You are so enthralled with the newness of the car. You are cruising around taking in the sights and sounds that are going on all around you.

People are looking at your car and you are busy looking back at them. So much so, that you fail to pay attention to the road signs and the gauges. Pretty soon you will either drive off the road from not paying attention to where you are going or you will run out of gas. And if you continue long enough without changing the oil, the engine will soon die.

If you have ever been in Driver's Education classes, one of the first things they teach you is this. It is critical that when you get behind the wheel of that car, you must give it your undivided attention. Destiny is a lot like that.

The minute you stop paying attention to the process of your destiny, you will begin to lose focus. You fail to notice the distractions that are on the side of the road. People fail in their recovery because of the same reasons. They forget they have to continually pay attention to their surroundings. The places they go, the people they hang out with. Some of those places and people may not be conducive to the health of their recovery.

This doesn't mean you have to lock yourself in the house, watch TBN and never speak to anybody. What it does mean is that you need to look after the welfare of your sobriety. You should do this just like you would look after the welfare of a toddler in your home. When your child starts to crawl and walk around the house it's time to baby-proof the house. You make sure the electrical outlets are covered and the cabinets are locked. You pay extra care and attention to what is around the house that could cause junior to get hurt.

There is an individual I know that came to get help from us many years ago. Even though he has been walking in recovery since he left, he remains diligent. He still gives his undivided attention to the little things that could distract him.

He doesn't carry a credit or debit card. He doesn't carry any more than five or ten dollars on him. He doesn't go out after dark by himself. If he has to go to the store after dark he will take someone with him and carry just enough money to get what he needs. In other words, he practices safe accountability. He has learned that his destiny calls for undivided attention in order for him to continue to walk in it.

Conclusion

In order to keep your destiny fresh in your heart you also need to be passionate about it. Earlier we talked about the seven words that keep you moving toward your destiny. One of those words was **sense**. We talked about how important it was to sense or feel the passion for what is in your heart. The things that you love doing, that just came natural. That is the essence of destiny.

Passion is the breath that gives life to your destiny. Without it you would soon lose interest and revert back to your old ways. In fact, without passion in your life, it is nearly impossible to stay motivated. Passion is the icing on the cake that allows you to give undivided attention to your destiny. Without it your destiny would just become another passing thought.

Passion is what enables me to do what I do day in and day out. Without it I would have gotten bored and left a long time ago. To me, there is nothing that gives me more passion than seeing lives transformed on a daily basis. It is what gives me the strength to get up every morning and go to work.

How do you know what you're passionate about? You have to find that idea or place that makes you lose sleep at night. Whatever you are passionate about will consume your thoughts on a regular basis. You can't escape it. It is with you wherever you go. Any time you have a spare minute to think you get lost in thought just thinking about your passion.

Everyone has a natural passion. Passion is what causes you to stand up yell at the TV during football season when your favorite team is playing. Passion is what causes you to go to work every day so you can provide a living for your family. Passion is what drives you to have a daily devotion with God. You do this because you know that is the strength that keeps you sane in an insane world. Passion will cause you do things for God that you might never do. Things that would've caused you embarrassment before you came to know Jesus.

What we have to do to maintain our destiny is use this passion to keep things new and fresh. It has been said that familiarity breeds contempt. The things that we love in the beginning are despised in the end when we get used to them. We must never lose sight of what God has done for us. He has brought us from a desert so vast that there is no hope for us if we ever go out there again.

I know that right now some of you are so excited you can barely contain yourselves. You have caught a glimpse of what your legacy can be and you are ready to get started. But then, on the other hand, there are those of you that are so scared that you are shaking in your shoes. You are looking at your life and can't even imagine anything good you can leave behind for others to follow.

The good thing for both of you is that it doesn't matter where you were in the past or where you are right now. You can change that by starting today. The choices you make starting right now will affect the rest of your life. Those choices will determine the legacy you will leave behind.

So start this new journey with a fresh sense of joy and renewal. You are embarking on a new life that will take you places you had only dreamed of before now. Take the time to focus on your journey and not be so consumed with everything around you. It is true that we need to aim at something or we will hit nothing. But it is also true that you can let your senses come alive as you enjoy the process that will get you to your destination.

If you understand your destiny, you will not have a hard time being passionate about it. You will be able to walk in the supernatural with undivided attention. If you do this, then your journey is a joy. Once you discover the satisfaction that comes with instilling passion in your life. You will do everything in your power to uncover your passion.

Stay focused in the destiny God has called you to do. God is always on your side and will help you in completing the path He has chosen for you. Just trust in Him and realize that just waking up each morning to start a new day fresh is part of your destiny. Don't despise the little things. Embrace them as part of your journey and it will make things worthwhile in the end.

FOOTNOTES

[1] Smiley, Tavis. (n.d.). Legacy. Retrieved August 16, 2014, from https://www.goodreads.com/quotes/tag/legacy

[2] *The American Heritage® Dictionary of the English Language, Fourth Edition*. Houghton Mifflin Company, 2004. 20 Jul. 2009. <Dictionary.com http://dictionary.reference.com/browse/destiny>.

[3] Daniel G. Amen

[4] John Maxwell

[5] Unknown

M.A.P. Your SOULUTION

Make a Plan
- On a separate piece of paper or in your journal, write down what kind of a legacy you want to leave behind. Be as descriptive as possible. Not, "I want to inspire others." But more like, "I want to inspire others with my testimony of how they can accomplish _____ by doing _____."
- Also write down what you think your calling or what part of God's purpose He has called you to do (again, be descriptive).

Accept Accountability {Recruit Partner(s) to Keep You Focused}
- Share with someone you trust your results from above so they can hold you accountable.
- Ask several people to write down what they think your calling or purpose is.

Put it into Action
- If you don't have a H.S. Diploma or G.E.D. take the steps necessary to enroll in classes now. You can never have enough knowledge. If you do look into some local community college classes that will help you accomplish what you have written above.
- For each item you wrote above take a separate sheet of paper and make a pro vs con list. Share with your accountability.

NOTES

NOTES

ERADICATING SELF-SABOTAGE

"For the whole law is fulfilled in one word, in the statement, 'You shall love your neighbor as <u>yourself</u>.'"
Galatians 5:14

"In order to cultivate personal freedom people must confront their inner demons and overcome the <u>self-sabotage</u> of doubt, delay, and division."
Brendon Burchard,
The Motivation Manifesto

CHAPTER 7
INVOLVE

Connect to a Cause

"Truth never damages a cause that is just."
— *Mahatma Gandhi*[1]

"This is dumb and it's not what I came here to do. I'm leaving!" Those were the words that came out of John's mouth as he was leaving the program for the third time. John's life was not going in the direction he wanted. That was how he found his way into our program in the first place. But before we talk about his direction, we need to understand where he came from. He had broken the rules yet again and was not willing to face the consequences that were a result of his actions. John's response is not so different from the response you and I have had when faced with similar circumstances.

Saying that John came from a dysfunctional family is an understatement. He never had much to do with his biological father. He grew up with his step-dad, mother, sister and three brothers until he was fifteen. It was during that time John was molested by a male family member several times. This in turn led him to an identity crisis. He didn't know who he was. He didn't know how to connect with people.

As you can probably guess by now, John wound up living in an alternative lifestyle. It was a lifestyle that involved homosexuality, drugs and gang activity. He did try to go *"straight"* one time, but it

145

ended in a disaster. That encounter left him with several sexually transmitted diseases. This in turn, drove him deeper into the homosexual lifestyle. Drugs and alcohol were his constant companions.

So when he came to me, he had very little use for a male authority figure. In fact, we had several meetings where he made it plain that he had trouble with me in particular. This was because I represented a father figure that to him was a negative role model.

I am embarrassed to say that it came as no surprise to me, when he decided to leave. But then he came back, and then left, and then came back, and left. In reality, he left and came back for a total of about four times.

The last time he left I remember having a conversation with him. I told him something I hoped would create a desire in him. I said, "John, you will never find the ability to connect to what you're looking for on your own. You must allow God to complete what He has started in you."

A short while later he came back. This time, he not only completed the program, he ended up staying a second year as a volunteer in our office. He even wound up being hired as an administrative assistant to one of the ministries on campus. It was also during this time that he decided to go to Bible College. He felt a calling into ministry and wanted to get a Biblical foundation. He pursued that just as wholeheartedly as he had pursued his old lifestyle.

At the writing of this book John has now moved on to another city where he is actively involved in ministry. He works a full time job in the public service sector. He has had his own radio show where he highlighted ministries that were being effective in the town he lives in. Most recently, he has just started a new Dream Center in this same town. To say that I am proud of him is a gigantic understatement.

John's story is what this book is all about. It is about how God can take a life full of despair, hopelessness and bitterness, and then turn it all around through His transformation power. It is proof that love can and does change lives when all else fails.

The awesome part of all this is that I get to see this transformation take place on a regular basis. I get to see people's lives transformed right in front of me every single day. God is changing their lives.

He does this not only by His supernatural power. But, by also helping them conquer the chaos in their lives. He is at work connecting them to something much bigger than themselves. And, by helping people connect to their own cause, a by-product occurs. They are learning to escape from their own selfish lifestyle of addictions.

Involve Yourself In Something Bigger Than You

Alternative lifestyles were something I never had to deal with until coming to California. In fact, if you had asked me about alternative lifestyles before I came to California, I would have asked if it was a punk rock band. You could say that I lived a sheltered life. I was raised in Oklahoma, in the middle of the Bible belt. My family was a conservative middle-class family. We went to church every time the doors were open.

I was what most people considered, a good kid. I never caused any major problems at home or school. In fact, the only drug problem I ever had my entire life, was that I was "*drug*" to church every time the doors were opened. You might say that by today's standards, my life was boring. But it didn't seem that way to me at the time. I was happy with life and where I was. ⊡

In all actuality, the last place I ever expected to be was in California. I could never have imagined doing what I do now. I get to serve people who are recovering from addictions and other life-controlling problems.

The reason I felt it important to share this with you, is so you can understand the mindset that I came from. The plan I had for my life was way different than the plan God had for me. My dream was to be involved in a typical church, serving a typical congregation.

Little did I know that this was miles away from the plan that

God would have for my life. And never in my wildest dreams, would I have ever believed you telling me anything to the contrary. In fact, if you had told me that I would be doing what I am doing now I would have laughed in your face. Ministering to people coming out of alternative and addicted lifestyles is not something I desired to do.

This is why John's story is so close to my heart. Before I came to California, I had a close friend and mentor speak into my life. She felt led to tell me that God was calling me to have a father's heart toward a fatherless generation.

I personally believe that is why God uses me in this area. This is what sets this program apart from other mainstream recovery programs. God uses the anointing of a father's heart to restore them to His heart.

My desire is to make people feel as though they belong to something bigger than themselves. I want them to grasp an important truth. They are more than just another person in a residential, community setting. They are part of a family that is connected by a bond that goes deeper than blood.

When a person comes to us, they soon realize they are part of a family. We even joke about this and give them a comparison. "We are like the mafia, you are now family, once a disciple, always a disciple." They also get a sense that this is a safe place to be. It is a place to relax and let your hair down, so you can drop all the masks and just be yourself.

All that is possible because this is a place where the Father-heart is at work. God is helping to make dreams of restoration and success come true. It is by no means perfect, but it comforting for sure.

Today John is not just a former graduate of the program. To me, he is more like the son I never had. In fact, whenever we are together, he introduces me to his friends and acquaintances as his Dad. And when we call and talk to each other he calls me dad and I call him son. This usually raises quite a few eyebrows and is always fun to watch because I am Caucasian and John is Latino. But we are a family that has been brought together by a loving God that delights in diversity.

I also believe there is another part of the equation for success here. It is being under a great pastor that is different than most. Pastor Matthew Barnett is one of those individuals that make you feel special, just by being you.

He preached one of his signature sermons that have stuck with me for many years. It is simply titled; "Belong to Believe." The basic concept is that most churches want you to believe first then belong to them. But Pastor Matthew, or PMB as we call he here on campus teaches us something radically different. This teaching has become part of our DNA. It is in fact, the opposite of that. You must first belong to something before you can believe in it.

When you take a closer look at this concept, you will find that it is not something new. In fact, it is what Jesus taught us. When he called His disciples to follow Him, He didn't require them to go to Bible School or join the church first. He just matter-of-factly invited them to come and be part of something huge. They were a part of something God was using to transform the world. That is how I feel about the Discipleship recovery program.

This is one of the secrets of success in our program. We don't force religion or even a relationship upon people. For us, it is a natural by product of belonging to a cause that is greater than you. It never gets old seeing this happen on a daily basis. People come to us immersed in the selfish lifestyle of addictions. Then, little by little, they become involved in a culture of serving others. When you serve other that are less fortunate than you, a transformation begins to take place.

Suddenly, it is no longer about them. It is about how they get to serve other in a unique culture. This is a culture that is constantly focused on finding a hurt and healing it, finding a need and filling it. It changes the very core of who they are.

It creates an atmosphere of serving others without expecting anything in return. It shows the importance of building relationships with people. This is needed if you want to serve them even more. After all, isn't that what Jesus came to this earth for? To build a relationship with us so that He could serve us even more? That is the example He showed us. That is the example we are to live if we want to belong to Him.

Involve Yourself In Your Relationships

Knowing this is what will keep us connected to people even when they are unlovable. The reality of life is this; people are some of the most valuable assets that we can have in our life. Learning how to get along with them is crucial for our success.

But that is always the hard part, isn't it? It would be great if we were given an instruction manual on relationships. Think of what we knew how to do this successfully. We could establish and cultivate every relationship to its fullest potential. But, since we do not, it falls on us to try and figure things out as best we can.

Untold countless books have been written about this topic, but still we struggle in this area. A fellow minister and friend of mine once said, "Ministry would be fun if it weren't for all the messed up people." He of course was half-joking and half-serious. There was, however, a grain of truth in that statement.

On the other hand, relationships are the glue that holds us together. When you see lives transformed it is a sight to behold. You see them go from being messed up, to being cleaned up, right in front of your eyes. It will cause great joy in your soul when you witness this taking place.

Relationships are definitely a two-edged sword. I believe that most people don't want to be a hermit. They have no desire to live their life on a desolate mountain, far away from needy people. Although, I must admit, that proposition can be tempting to consider for a moment.

On the other hand, being surrounded by a multitude of people is not all joy either. This is especially true if they are constantly demanding all your attention. This is not something to be desired either. Developing a balanced view is necessary to maintain some degree of sanity. But how is that possible? How can you ignore a need that presents itself to you? Especially, when you know you don't have the strength to handle things at that moment?

The answer may be simpler than you think. It is important to understand that we were created for relationship, with each other and with God. This is necessary to be successful in life. Life is full of demanding, needy people that are looking for answers to their questions. We cannot ignore them and hope they will go away.

Neither can we allow a bitter root to spring up in our heart as a result of some past relationship gone sour. We must learn to love unconditionally like Jesus did. Look at what John had to say about this issue in 1 John 4:20. *"If someone says, 'I love God.' and hates his brother, he is a liar; for the one who does not love his brother whom he has seen, cannot love God, whom he has not seen."*

Acknowledging that we are not perfect and that we have flaws is uncomfortable at best. Adding other people into that mix can be the stuff nightmares are made of. The reality of it all is that we need each other. And, that is true even if you are struggling with life-controlling problems. It is also true if you are the friend, loved one or concerned caregiver of such a person, it makes no difference. God created us this way and it is pointless to fight it.

If you want make a difference in people's lives then you will have to connect with them. Hey, I heard that heavy sigh you just made. I even heard some of you say under your breath, "Do I have to?" The answer to that question is a simple, no. You don't have to learn how to live a life free from a ball and chain that you drag around everywhere you go.

You can continue to move from church to church once people find out who you are. You can continue to pretend that's just the way you are. You can even continue to blame your Uncle Joe, or whomever else you want to blame that it's not your fault. But you and I both know the truth. And the silly thing is, so does everybody else. So in reality you are not fooling anyone, not even yourself.

I can imagine some of you thinking to yourself right now; "What does he know about my life?" "What qualifies him to say such things?" Let me tell you a little more about myself. Even though, I may not have experienced some of the things that you have, I have a story. I can relate to what you're going through. I know you may think that a bold statement coming from someone like myself, but stick with me for a moment. I believe that God has given me some supernatural understanding on this. It will help you conquer the chaos in your life.

The problem is not the addiction or whatever you're using to cover your pain. Those are merely symptoms. In sixteen years of doing recovery ministry I have found that these life-controlling issues can most often be traced back to one thing; pain. Pain, that most likely stems from a warped view of a father figure in your life, or the lack thereof. And when I say, "warped" I'm not necessarily talking about a negative father figure. One of the definitions of warped is; "to distort or cause to distort from the truth, fact, true meaning, etc."[2]

You father could have been just like mine and worked two jobs most of my life. Most of the memories I have of personal, one-on-one interaction between my father and myself are few and far between. Don't get me wrong, he was a great provider and I know that he loved me. But because of his job, he was rarely ever there. And because of that, my view of God as a Father to me was different than what God intended for me.

I saw God the Father as a far away Provider that I only approached to get permission to do something. I didn't see him as a Father that deeply longed to have a personal, intimate relationship with me. My father taught me a lot by about work ethics and being a person of character. But, he taught me very little in relationship issues. I don't blame him. He didn't know how to because that is what he learned from his father. And I would assume that is what my grandfather learned from his own father as well.

In order for me to learn how to connect better with God, I had to have a radical shift in my viewpoint. I had to have a vision of who God; the Father, really was to me. And, if you want a radical difference in your life, then you must do the same. You must get radical about the changes that need to take place in your life as well. That is what this book is all about.

Let's face the truth here for a minute. If there were some other program that had a 100% cure rate, you would have tried it by now. If there were some self-help book with all the answers, you would have already bought it by now. If you or the loved one in your life were struggling, you would've already tried everything by now.

If that were the case, you would not be reading through this book. You would not be frantically searching the pages for some glimmer of hope. But, you are looking for something fresh. You want something different. You need an alternative viewpoint, if you will. One that will deliver you or your loved one from the bondage that has been a living nightmare. Why not try connecting to a relationship with Jesus. He just might surprise you as you connect to Him!

Involve Yourself In Your Responsibility

Accepting responsibility is something we have struggled with since the dawn of creation. When caught in his sin, all Adam could do was blame the woman that God gave him. Likewise, Eve followed suit by blaming the serpent that God had created. Are you beginning to see the pattern here?

From the very beginning of our existence we have been shifting blame. Instead of taking responsibility for our actions, we will choose to blame someone else. Some people will make excuses and will call it a defense mechanism or self-preservation. But it is usually the result of some deeply rooted problem that we are trying to hide. Psychology experts call it deflecting. We will point out someone else's weakness to shift the blame away from ourselves. We want to prevent anyone from finding out that we have problems.

Acknowledging that we are wrong or even have a problem can be difficult to admit. It is something that God has been trying to do since He established the whole plan of restoration. Soon after the fall of Adam in the Garden of Eden, God was at work. He was busy orchestrating his grand plan of reestablishing an intimate relationship with us. Even Jesus made mention of his desire for relationship in Luke 13:34 NLT. *"Oh Jerusalem...How often I have wanted to gather your children together as a hen protects her chicks beneath her wings, but you wouldn't let me."*

Developing an understanding of why we act this way is an even more difficult concept to process. We act as if our love is a toy that we hoard like a spoiled child. When faced with the prospect of sharing it with another child, we throw a temper tantrum. Then we are aware that what we are doing is not what we really want to do. And, if the truth is made known, deep inside we are longing for someone to share this moment with us. Why we do this is somewhat of a mystery. It may take many years of counseling to find out that you have a problem of accepting responsibility. And, that in turn creates problems with relationships.

Connecting with others is what we were made for. We were created to be relational beings. That is why we feel so empty and alone when there is no one to share things with. We desire for someone to share our celebrations with. We need a shoulder to cry on to share our disappointments with. That is why addictions and other life-controlling problems are so destructive. They cause us to first disconnect from reality, then with people, until we are all alone.

When a person is enveloped in a lifestyle of responsibility avoidance, it is difficult to overcome. The only thing they want is to be completely free. They are longing for freedom from the emotional pain they have been experiencing. This could be pain from a traumatic event that happened at some point in their life. I refer to this as an activating event in a person's life.

However, I have come to the conclusion that the pain may go much deeper than that. It is usually coupled with the betrayal of a close relationship. The aftermath of which, has often left them scarred and handicapped. Their ability to develop relationships is damaged. These types of suffering will habitually manifest itself in a variety of issues. This will lead to continued, negative behaviors. These behaviors, will then lead individuals down a sometimes dangerous and destructive path. They won't to avoid the responsibility and the pain that goes with it, at any cos.

So then, what is the answer to all this? I wish there was a simple explanation that would make all the pain go away. Sadly, there is not. It is a long road back to complete healing and restoration. I know we live in an age of quick fixes, but the reality of this is that you didn't get this way overnight. It will take more than a mere twenty-eight days to fix something like this.

The starting point connecting with responsibility is being willing to confess and accept blame. You must own up for what you have done. There is a freedom that comes with this action that I have no words to explain. It goes into the very depth of our soul. When we accept responsibility we are connecting to a higher power. That power is Jesus. He gives us power to make right choices and turn our life around. But none of that can even start until we admit our part in it.

There is a good reason why that is the first step in the twelve steps of Alcoholics Anonymous. Because, if you can't admit that you have a problem, then basically, in your mind, you don't. And you will never receive the help you need to overcome the problems in your life.

It takes real courage to admit the truth of what you are struggling with and that you have no control in your life. Your only step at that point is to give up and turn things over to God. He knows the truth. He understands the truth, but most importantly, He is waiting for you to confess the truth.

Involve Yourself In The Truth

Since we've already established that the choices we make determine our direction for life. Then we can also surmise that not all choices will lead us to the destination that we had hoped for. In fact, for most of us, the choices we have made, rarely ever point us in the direction of our destiny.

Why is this? Is there something within us that rebels at the very thought of doing the right thing? Why do we cringe at making consistently right choices? Is there still hope for those of us that

155

want to turn our lives around? How do we bring ourselves to admit that we have been wrong and have made bad choices? Is there any way to get off of this roller coaster of insanity and get our feet back on solid ground?

At this point, I feel it is necessary to encourage you to realize that you can recover. It is possible to get your life back and going in the right direction again. We have all made a mess of our lives at one time or another. But in spite of our shortcomings there remains something within us that drives us to believe for more. It is to reach for something better than the life we are now living! Being open and honest with you is the first step in this process. It is not easy to determine the right direction, but it is possible.

It is essential that you connect to people that care about you. They must have a legitimate interest in your well-being. It is also a good first step on your road to connect with the truth. Look, we've all been at the end of a bad relationship before. The only way out of the mess we've made is to turn our lives around and admit that we were wrong. It is never easy admitting we were wrong. No one likes to admit that they made a mistake. And some of us have made some pretty bad mistakes. But it is necessary.

But the truth is elusive. The road to truth is filled with secrets. Secrets, such as; "Why are we always trying to feel good?" or "Why do we always have to go from one thrill to the next?" Just exactly what is the truth we are trying so hard to hide through all these lame excuses? I know that is a tough question, and may not seem fair. But you may find a surprise when you answer that question. You will not only discover the truth that has been so elusive, you will also see the lies that have been hiding that truth.

What you do with the truth is also just as important as discovering it. For example, suppose you find out that a very close friend of yours is about to commit suicide. The logical choice that you should make would be to call the authorities and alert them to what is about to happen. You might instead decide to go to where your friend is and do an intervention yourself. Or, in some cases, you might simply decide to do nothing. You surmise that your friend is a grown adult and he is responsible for his own actions. It is not your problem, or is it?

I would suggest to you that when you decide to connect with people, that philosophy goes out the window. You are also deciding that if you connect, you are responsible enough to look out for their safety. However, the previous scenario is played out countless times each day. In the addictions arena, suicide may not be the intended desire of the people in question. But the effects of their decision can be just as deadly. Since I have been working in recovery ministry, I have seen this firsthand. There have been a few instances of individuals that have left prematurely. These folks have found themselves back in their addictions and ultimately to their deaths.

While I am almost certain this was not their plan, it happened anyway. They did not act on the truth they had discovered for their lives. They failed to realize an important aspect of recovery; you can't do it alone! You need other people to connect with and give you the motivation you need to make it through the tough times. You need other people to be real with you and share the truth with you, even though it may be hard to accept. That is what real friends do. That is how you act when you have made a decision to connect with a cause that is greater than you.

Conclusion

What is your cause that is bigger than you? I am talking about something that is bigger than you could ever do on your own. Because if you can do it all by yourself, it is not something bigger than you, is it? It's not a God dream. You were born for greatness. You were placed on this earth to be connected to something great that God put you here to do. And, it will only be accomplished by connecting to the cause associated with that task.

Contrary to the belief of our society, the universe does not revolve around you. You are not the center of everything. Only God holds that title. The fact is, that most people who struggle with addictions, are very selfish. Finding a cause to believe in will help take the focus off of you and your problems. It will help you begin to look at how you can give of yourself instead of always being a taker.

I must admit to you that this is not something that comes quickly or easily to other people like yourself. It takes a lot of practice, hard work, and of course; accountability. I know some of you made a face at that last word. But, accountability is absolutely necessary for your success. In order to keep moving forward, you must walk out your *SOULUTIONS*!

FOOTNOTES

[1] Gandhi, M. (n.d.). Causes. . Retrieved July 10, 2014, from
https://www.goodreads.com/quotes/search?commit=Search&page=2&q
=causes&utf8=⬚

[2] http://dictionary.reference.com/browse/warp?s=t

M.A.P. Your SOULUTION

Make a Plan
- Take a few minutes to write down what you feel your cause (something you are passionate about) is.
- Next to that write down the following; what about your cause makes you willing to commit to it and will it meet the criteria of the four points mentioned in this chapter?

Accept Accountability {Recruit Partner(s) to Keep You Focused}
- Ask your accountability partner(s) what they see that you are passionate about and why, that could be classified as a cause.
- Ask a family member that knows you well the same question. Hopefully this confirms what you are already feeling. If it does not ask several people the same thing to determine if there is a pattern that you can see that will lead you to your cause.

Put it into Action
- Once you find out about your cause, find someplace that is already doing work along the same cause and volunteer some time with them.
- This is a very important step, as it will begin to polish your gifts in this area.

NOTES

NOTES

CHAPTER 8

ORDER

Choose Your Consistency

"Until a person can say, 'I am what I am because of the choices I made yesterday.' They cannot say, 'I choose otherwise.'"[1]
— *Dr. Stephen Covey*

All of his life, Tim never really knew who God was. He went to Sunday school as a child but in his mind it was just a place to get away from home for the day. In his early teens he went to a small church because they had a rock band, but before and after service he would smoke pot behind the church.

His mother and father separated when he was eight years old and from that time on, he didn't have much of a family life. As a result, he never really knew how to develop a relationship with anyone, or even God, for that matter. His mother had to work a lot to take care of him and his brothers. So, by the time he was fifteen it was just she and he in a small apartment. Eventually Tim started selling marijuana and L.S.D. and began using drugs a lot. His mother had no idea as she was still working all the time. When he was eighteen, his mother decided that she was going to finally live her life for herself for once and moved to Atlanta, GA.

Tim found himself on his own and continued to support himself by selling drugs until he was offered a job building warehouse systems traveling around the country. He had no responsibilities or anything tying him down to stop him from going so he went. He was now legit and in control of his own destiny. After traveling around for a while, he decided to stay in one place for some time. So he began to work in clubs as a bouncer. He started singing with a band and began to live life in the fast lane. This eventually got him a job at a strip club. However, it wasn't long before he started using and selling drugs again.

One night in late December he ran into a girl who used to work for him. It was about 4 am and she offered to pay him to give her and her boyfriend a ride to Orlando. So they went on a wild road trip, smoking crack and pot. They were shooting up with cocaine, and partying the whole way. They ended up on a road in a not so nice area of Orlando. The next thing he knew there were four guns pointed at his head and he was being robbed for everything he had. They took his drugs, his money, they even took a shoebox he had with all the pictures of his daughter in it. So here he was in a city he had never been to before. He had no money, no gas in his car and no way to get back home.

Through a series of miraculous events, Tim encountered three different people within a three-day period that changed his life. As he encountered each of them at different times and circumstances they all said the same thing. That where he was at now was a direct result of the choices he'd made and what he had been doing. In fact, all of their exact words were; "You ain't got no one to blame but yourself and that it was up to him to choose to change his life." This really freaked him out, as he hadn't told any of them where he was from or what had happened to him so he started looking for a church. He just wanted to get home and forget about this whole ordeal. He couldn't find an open church so he just wondered around until he fell asleep at a park on a bench.

The next day Tim found a phone and called his sister. She told him that her mother would put a bus ticket on line for him. He arrived home and attempted to change his life after that. He quit selling cocaine and using. He totally changed everything except he continued to work in the strip clubs because it was easy money. His life started to be normal again. He had everything he wanted out of life but still there was something missing.

Within about three years Tim started using cocaine again. It was just a little to begin with, but soon it got worse and eventually his relationships started to suffer because of it. He kept his cocaine use hidden from his everyone. One day Tim got in his friend's car. As soon as he sat down, his friend handed him a bag full of crack and said, "Just let go and get high." So he did. Tim had his friend drop him off at a hotel and bought $3,600 worth of crack and attempted to smoke it all until he died. He stayed in that room for two days and no matter how much he smoked he wouldn't die. He couldn't figure out why.

The following Monday Tim went to work and turned in his two weeks' notice. At the end of the two weeks, he packed up all his stuff and bought a one-way bus ticket to L.A. He got a hotel room in Jacksonville for the weekend. That Saturday night as he went to dinner with some friends, his hotel room got broken into and the money that he had saved for his trip was stolen. That was all the money he had to go to California on. His friends tried to talk him out of going. They told him that he was crazy to go to California with no money. But for some reason Tim felt compelled to go any way.

He got on the bus with $10.00 in his pocket and rode three days until he got to L.A. He arrived without his luggage so he waited until the next day to see if it would arrive. It didn't. Finally the people at the bus station told him that he couldn't stay there anymore and had to leave. So he started walking in the direction he thought was Hollywood. Tim walked around L.A. for three days. He pawned his guitar, hoping that would get him enough money for a hotel room, but it wasn't.

After the third day of sleeping on the beach, with no food, no shower, and no idea of what he was going to do, Tim became really distraught. He actually thought to himself that he would sell his soul to get out of this hole and get on his feet or become famous. He spent his last three dollars on a bus pass and headed to Hollywood from Santa Monica.

While he was on the bus he met two ladies sitting next to him. During their conversation he told them about his ordeal and how that he hadn't had a shower or eaten in days. One of the ladies asked him if he had ever heard of the "Dream Center"? He said "No, what's the Dream Center?" She then told him that the other woman was her daughter and that she was a volunteer at this place and that they had a discipleship program.

Tim had no idea what a discipleship program was so he asked, "What's that?" and what she said next sent chills down his spine. She told him that it was a place where he could learn to serve God and be a better person. This was exactly what he had prayed for three weeks prior. It was like a giant bell went off in his head and he said "Please take me there." All of a sudden, he felt a calm come over him like he knew in his heart that everything was going to be all right.

Needless to say, Tim graduated the program and became part of the leadership team. He even stayed on as a second year volunteer to give back and pour into others just as he had been poured into. Today Tim has more joy and peace in his heart than he has ever known. Since he has come to know Jesus, he has learned the meaning of true servant hood, and how to study the Bible.

Today, Tim is free from the addictions of cocaine, marijuana, and nicotine that he had when he came to get help from us. Now that he knows the right path to follow, he can see no other way. Now that he understands what a life of serving God is like there is no reason for him to go back to the old lifestyle that he has left behind.

Order Your Transformation

Our society is filled with clichés when comes to talking about the lack of our ability to change. At some point, someone, somewhere, will hear sayings like; *"The apple doesn't fall very far from the tree."* or *"A leopard can't change its spots."* or my all time favorite; *"You can't teach an old dog new tricks."* I think that if you have tried to change before you have heard someone say this about you.

It seems as if our society is stuck on the fact that change is next to impossible to accomplish. There is an underlying belief that most of us are doomed to an existence of just settling for living life as it is. Despite our best efforts, it seems as if we will never be able to break free of the chains that keep us from experiencing true and lasting change. You get up, go to work, and try to do the right things, and then something bad happens to you again. It's like the universe is against you no matter how hard you try to do well. If you find yourself stuck here, don't beat yourself up too bad because there are many other people stuck in the same boat.

This is where I really want you to give me your full attention. In spite of all this, you need to know that change does happen and it occurs quite frequently and consistently on a regular basis. The greatest change of all takes place when you choose to change your life completely by surrendering your struggle and giving it over to God. You can become a new person by accepting the transformation that Jesus has to offer you. This makeover; from the old to the new, is clearly life changing. The Apostle Paul describes it this way; *"Therefore, if anyone is in Christ, he is a new creation; the old has gone, the new has come!"* – 2 Corinthians 5:17 NIV

Countless individuals have asked me the question; "So tell me, is it really possible for someone like me to change?" My response to them is always the same. I look them right in the eyes, usually through my own tears and tell them; "Not only is real change possible, I have seen it happen thousands of times over the last fifteen or so years. You just have to find the right reason as to why you want to change, and the right soulution to help make that change possible."

Real, lasting change can only occur when there is a climate favorable for change. Only you can determine that for yourself. It involves a lot more than just wanting to be a better person. If it were that easy we wouldn't have all the problems we have today. It involves being consistent to yourself and the transformation that you have chosen to do. But that is not all there is to it.

You must choose to follow through on these decisions so

167

people know you mean business. My guess is that you may have tried doing this already, but because you burned a lot of bridges in your life over the years, found it difficult to accomplish. If I am right about this, then it is time to do something different. It is time to move on to the next step.

Let me give you a revelation. You can't transform yourself no matter how hard you try. The reason is; true transformation is an inside job. This is why so many people get frustrated at this point in their recovery. They try and try and try and still struggle with success. They begin to believe something is wrong with them and they deserve the problems they are struggling with. This is why self-sabotage is so prevalent at this point.

Don't get me wrong here. You do have a part to play in the transformation process. You are the only one that can choose when you are ready to change. Then, once you have made that decision, you have to take on the attitude of a caterpillar. The caterpillar reaches a point in its life to where it cannot grow any more.

There are too many distractions in its life. So it must build a cocoon around itself so that God can begin the transformation process in its life. It goes into this process as a lowly worm that crawls around until it gets tired of where it is at in life. It then surrenders itself to the lonely process of being alone with God and comes out as a beautiful creature that commands the sky. It has been transformed into a completely different creature. The old is gone and the new has just begun. But, like I said earlier, you have your part to play in this.

Order Your Actions

You have to come to a point in your life where you decide that you are ready to choose something different. You must be tired of crawling around on the ground and being stepped on by everybody. When you finally get to that point, you are ready to take command of your actions. It's now time to start making right choices.

You have to separate yourself from the distractions that have brought you down. You can't continue in the same existence if you want to be changed. You must order yourself to start a new journey for your life. It's time for you to become free from your self-imposed boundaries.

The definition for insanity has been described as doing the same thing over and over again while expecting different results. I'm sure you've found yourself repeating some of the same things in your life and thinking, it will be different this time. The answer is usually always the same.

You find yourself right back into your mess again, if not worse than before. You see if you really want to change your life, you must choose to change what you're doing. You have to take actions that start moving you in a new direction.

Some people tend to get bent out of shape when they think about changing their whole life around. But change is unavoidable. It is also a normal and healthy part of life. It's not as difficult as you're imagining it to be. Let me give you an example. Have you ever gotten tired of the way you looked and wanted to change? You looked around one day and noticed that the styles were changing. If you wanted to be with the 'in' crowd, then you needed to change your 'style' as well.

Just stay with that thought for a minute more. I know you might be thinking; "That's ridiculous, what does that have to do with my problem?" Just think about this for a moment. You wanted to change, so you looked at where you were, then looked at where you wanted to be and made a decision to go there. You didn't have to involve a committee or go around asking people what you should do. You just made a decision and did it. It's just that simple to change. However, we tend to complicate this process with all of our excuses.

Let me illustrate this for you. Using this line of thinking as an example you might come up with some excuses. One might be; "My hair is so difficult to work with, I'm not sure what it would look like with a new style." Or still yet, "What's wrong with the way I look and the clothes I wear?" Are you beginning to see what I'm talking about yet? We may want change but we don't want to go through the process to get there because it is inconvenient. But eventually, you reach a place to where the desire to change is greater than the inconvenience.

Now, stay with me for just a bit more. The next step is where most people fail to engage. If you really want to change then you have to put action to your desires. You have to decide that you are willing to pay the price for change. You have to go shopping and buy new clothes, or go to the beauty salon to change your hairstyle.

Or even better yet; tell someone else what you want to do so they will help you follow through. Someone that you trust and won't make fun of you and will even help you find the right hair stylist. The point of the example is this. Change first starts in your mind. We think in pictures not words. So, if you want to change then you first have to see a picture, in your mind, of what you want to be.

Many things in today's society can influence you and paint pictures in your mind. In the example I just gave to you. You would have most likely have been influenced by celebrities. Such as what the latest movie star is wearing, or how they fixed their hair? On top of that, you probably began seeing other people wearing the same style of clothes or the same hairdo. The simple truth of the matter is this; you were coerced by your surroundings to make a lifestyle change.

If you want to make this kind of a lifestyle change then you need to change your surroundings. Things like; the places you go, the people you hang out with, etc., etc. You can't keep doing the same thing and expect different results it just won't work. If you want to be transformed like the caterpillar; you have to get away from what is familiar to you. You must inconvenience yourself in order to be transformed into something else, something beautiful. This same principle that works for the caterpillar is also true for you.

Order Your Atmosphere

All of the above works together towards one end. That is to

create an atmosphere of change in your mind. An atmosphere is set by the way you respond to certain influences on a consistent basis. You didn't get trapped into your problems overnight. You began by setting an atmosphere that was conducive to change. You started hanging around certain people because they were fun to be with.

Then you wanted to be more accepted so you started doing some of the same things they were doing. Eventually, you found yourself compromising in order to fit in with your new friends. It was a gradual change that took place by your consistency in this area of your life. And then, this new atmosphere, then turned into a prison that you could not escape.

It's important to set an atmosphere because some things grow better in certain atmospheres. If you look at a tall mountain there is an imaginary line known as a tree line. This is where the atmosphere is so thin that even trees can't grow there. Another example to the extreme would be a fish. Fish can't live without being in the water. Their whole physiology is designed to extract what they need for life through the water. You and I on the other hand, could not survive in the water without some kind of breathing apparatus.

So, if you want to change the environment you are in, you must change your atmosphere. How do you change your atmosphere? I know that is probably the question burning on your mind right now. An atmosphere is set when you respond to certain conditions with regular consistency. In other words, you must have a predetermined plan on how you are going to react. You must set this up before you are faced with obstacles to your goal.

When your atmosphere is set just right, everything grows and flourishes. When your atmosphere is sustained over a long period of time it becomes a climate. Climates in time, makes environments or cultures. That may be where you find yourself right now. You may be in a culture of selfishness, abuse, dysfunction, life-controlling problems, etc.

Change begins to take place when you develop a counter-culture mindset. Your concept of culture will determine the level of freedom you will operate at. I believe that your identity is, for the most part, formed by your culture. Example: if you are Caucasian, Hispanic or African American your belief in whom you are as a person will have been greatly influenced by your ethnicity. Obviously, there are other factors that influence you as well, but this becomes a foundation that you build from.

As humans created in the image of God, we tend to be goal-oriented. Our ultimate goal is to make Heaven our home when we depart this life. Goals are also an important part of your culture. If your culture believes that you can never achieve a certain level of success then you will not. You will be in bondage to that belief or atmosphere until you change your thinking or your culture. And you do that by developing a plan that will take you where you want to go one step at a time.

But first you must have a goal. There is always a solution to every problem. We just don't always see it. Our minds become clouded by excuses about why we can't stop doing a particular thing. Our emotions, are perhaps more addictive, than any other thing you can think of. But once you choose to open up your mind to the possibility of success, then it has a chance to grow. No matter how bad the situation may look. You can choose to be consistent and make it happen.

Anything is possible in the realm of faith. Instead of using the phrase "seeing is believing" we must change our vocabulary. We must learn to use the phrase; "believing is seeing." This can be accomplished by looking for ways to exercise your faith. That is really what Paul meant in Hebrews 11:1 NLT when he said; "*What is faith? It is the confident assurance that what we hope for is going to happen. It is the evidence of things we cannot yet see.*"

It is hard to change the way you see things in life. Just as it is hard to go from one atmosphere to another, you must take time to adjust to the new climate. If you don't, then you will find it hard to breathe. You will find it difficult to be able to do the things you were meant to do until you adjust to your new atmosphere. But

172

once you do, you have discovered a whole new world of possibilities.

Order Your Options

When it comes to consistency, you generally don't think that options are available. But in the context of change, it is very much a part of being consistent. You are faced with options every day. And, everyday, you must choose to maintain the consistency of your sobriety. You do this by choosing the right options. It is not easy but it is something that must me done in order to walk in your S.U.C.C.E.S.S.

When you are consistent in your walk it allows you to gauge your success. If you are not consistent in doing something, you will never know if it truly works. You can't be 'one and done' to be consistent. You must keep at it until you can measure whether or not it is working. This is not a short process. It can take anywhere from three to six months to figure out if a particular pathway is working for you.

Consistency also creates accountability. And I am huge on accountability. It is, in my opinion, what makes the world go around. You need to establish an accountability team. It is a group of people who will help you mastermind your success in any given area.

Let me clear something up about accountability. Accountability is not just for calling somebody when you are thinking about doing something stupid. In order for it to work, you must have regular meetings with your accountability partner(s). They must be available to you and you must be available to them in order for this to work.

When you are looking at options for consistency, it is a good idea to think about your reputation. Some of you have ruined relationships because of your previous actions or lack thereof. You need to reestablish your consistency. You can't establish stability in your life if you are inconsistent. If you are currently going back and forth with your decision, you are inconsistent. You must maintain the course even if it looks like it is not making a difference.

The truth of the matter is this; it does make a difference. People are watching you. They are watching to see if you are going to make right choices. They want to see you work on rebuilding your reputation as a person that can be trusted again. They are also watching you to see if you are the same person in public as you are in private. You cannot be double minded and have S.U.C.C.E.S.S.

Another thing that goes along with your reputation is relevance. You have to be relevant to where people are living. You can't keep going down memory land, reminiscing about the 'good old days'. If you are trying to change your lifestyle, you must develop new memories. Think about this for a minute. If the 'good old days' were so good, then why aren't you still living in the 'good old days?'

Things change. People change. Times change. If you are to be steadfast in your transformation, you must change as well. If people are going to depend upon you again, you must be relevant and meet people where they are. It's not just about you anymore.

Finally, you must choose to uphold your message with your reliability. You are now in the business of communicating a brand new lifestyle to people. You have a message of hope to communicate. It is now, more than ever, about being reliable in that message.

People are watching. People that you have wronged. People that you used to hang out with. People are looking for a miracle. People that need to know they can have hope in their lives once again. And finally, people that need to see you are going to make it. People need to know that what you are saying and living, will work for them. Let your message be so radically reliable that everyone can see what God has done in your life.

Conclusion

You weren't born into this world with a life-controlling habit. There was, in fact, a time in your life that you didn't suffer from the consequences of drugs or alcohol. Can you remember that time? If you can't right now, that's okay. You just need to know that your restoration is going to be amazing. It will be more radical than anything that has ever happened in your life to this point.

You can now enjoy a life of freedom. What is it that you enjoy doing? The world is full of many wonderful things and experiences. Now is the time to restore old activities that were lost due to your selfish cravings. You may even want to find new things to do and explore. It's your life; you decide how to make the most of it!

Drug addiction today has a new face. It's not always the typical junkie in the street doing whatever they can to get high. It now claims doctors, nurses, housewives, business people, and teens. What's even more disturbing is that many of these people can function fairly well. They are able to hide their problems from most everyone.

Maybe you have found yourself struggling with an addiction. You are ready for some hope of a sober, drug-free life. If that is you, then you can start today! Take action right now! Don't wait any longer! It's time for you to do something now to begin your road to restoration. Even if it's just working yourself up in choosing what your desire in life is.

My hope is that you open yourself to the concepts and ideas that are being presented to you. They are life changing and have already changed thousands of lives over the course of the last sixteen years. I know you are curious and have lots of questions so let's continue shall we by mapping your SOULUTION below?

FOOTNOTES

[1] *The 7 Habits of Highly Effective People,* Covey, Stephen R. (Electronic Edition, © 2013, Rosetta Books, LLC.)

M.A.P. Your SOULUTION

Make a Plan
- What is one thing that you are struggling with about being consistent right now? Write in down on a piece of paper.
- Make sure you only wrote down one thing. Next, underneath it, write down the things you are doing that contribute to inconsistency in this one thing.
- Repeat this process as things come up that are showing inconsistency in your life. Only one thing at a time.

Accept Accountability {Recruit Partner(s) to Keep You Focused}
- Now I want you to go to your accountability partners, one at a time, and without showing them your list, ask them the same questions about yourself.
- After you have compiled a list of things, go back to them and ask them to hold you accountable in these areas by using the plan you make below.

Put it into Action
- Go through the lists you have made above. Now go through each item you listed where you contributed to inconsistencies in your life.
- For each contributing thing, I want you to write one paragraph of something you can do to change this behavior. Only do one thing at a time and enlist your accountability to help you.

NOTES

NOTES

CHAPTER 9

NEUTRALIZE

Eliminate Your Excuses

"Most people don't have that willingness to break bad habits.
They have a lot of excuses and they talk like victims."
— Carlos Santana[1]

Jim's father had died when he was eleven years old. During the most crucial time of his life, where a little boy is learning to become a man, he did not have an example to guide him. Jim was into sports, it kept him out of trouble and he was really good at just about any sport.

However, as he got older he began to have a desire to do something for God. He wasn't quite sure what that was but as he got more involved with his youth group he felt he was being called into ministry. This calling eventually led to him going to a Bible college after he graduated from High School.

For a while, life was great. He was doing well in school and was enjoying the blessings that God was giving to him. He was on top of his game and was enjoying the journey on his way to full-time ministry. He was looking forward to doing great things for God and leaving his mark on the world.

But, even in a Bible college there are elements that are not, shall we say, biblical. Jim eventually fell in with some of those people. This led him on a downhill spiral far away from a life of ministry. It was also during this time that he began to rely upon excuses as the blame for his poor decisions.

After all, if he had had a father in his life like normal people, he wouldn't have had to deal with all these hardships he was now going through. He started drinking to ease his pain. Which led to him making more excuses in order to cover up his behavior. He became a pathological liar. He could charm the socks off of anyone he came in contact with. He even got me a few times.

But as they say, all things must come to an end. And things eventually caught up with Jim. He was drinking one night and while he was driving he had an accident. Rather than waiting for the cops to come, he decided to run. Obviously, you can't run forever and he was arrested for felony hit and run. As a result of this he was expelled from Bible College.

After doing some time in jail, his mom sent him to a faith-based rehab similar to the Dream Center Discipleship program. He did very well there, for a time. Like I said previously, he was a charmer. But ultimately his true nature came out, as did the excuses for his actions. Needless to say, he was asked to leave that program.

He went home to live but by this time his mom had remarried and Jim and his stepdad did not get along very well. He did well for a while and stayed out of trouble. But just like the scripture says in James; "...a double-minded man is unstable in all his ways..." so too was Jim. He was given an ultimatum to come to our program or be on the streets.

When he first came here, he was a perfect example of an ideal client. He did everything right, at least on the surface, and had a lot of people fooled. Then one day, he was caught in a compromising situation with one of the girls in our program. Rather than own up to his mistakes, he again made excuses and blamed everyone but himself. He decided to leave.

However, after about a month, he decided to come back. This time things were different. He had a new attitude and a new approach on life. He came face to face with his excuses and realized that he couldn't use them as a crutch anymore. If he was to move forward in life, he had to eliminate them from his life and just trust God while being vulnerable at the same time. That was not easy for Jim, as he had spent the majority of his life making excuses for his behavior.

He finally caught a vision of who God created him to be. It rocked his world. He didn't have to make excuses because God loved him for who he was. It was an encounter I will never forget.

Jim moved on with his life and is now married with a couple of kids. I wouldn't say that his life is perfect but he is learning to let go and let God provide him with the **SOULUTIONS** he needs to continually move forward in life. And if you really want to move forward with your life then you need to do the same thing.

If you are reading this and can relate to Jim then you need to get rid of the excuses in your life. It's time for you start taking the blame for what you have created in your life. No one else can change you but you. And only you can make a decision to start fresh right now.

But you have to start. And you might as well start by doing something hard. This will probably be one of the hardest things that I have asked you to do so far. If you really want to change then you must do exactly what I'm telling you to do right now. You have to kick the *H.E.L.L.* out of yourself.

Ok, if you're really religious then that probably offends you. But before you get all upset and close the book, I'm not really cussing. You see H.E.L.L. is an acronym I'm using to drive home a point. So if you're still with me, keep reading and you'll find out what I'm talking about.

Neutralize Your Hate

The "H" in *H.E.L.L.* stands for Hate. I can only imagine what some of you may be thinking right now; "Hate is such a strong emotional word!" or "Is it really necessary to use that word?" I will prove my point if you will give me a few minutes here.

In John 3:20 NLT, we can read; *"All who do evil hate the light and refuse to go near it for fear their sins will be exposed."* The original meaning here is; "to detest (especially to persecute); by extension, to love less."[2] So as you can see, it is meant to be an emotionally strong word in this context.

Please keep in mind that these are the words of Jesus. He is trying to explain the process of being born again to an unbeliever. In this particular verse He is explaining why people do what they do and the reason why they choose not to accept a new life in Christ. It is quite simply because they hate the light and what it represents.

This can be a pretty big problem because the scripture tells us that Jesus is light. It is easy to keep things hidden where things cannot be seen. In other words, it is easy to make excuses when no one can see what you are really doing in the dark. This is the reason why Jesus said that those who are evil hate the light. As I previously stated above, the meaning can be two-fold; "to love less."

I would even extend this out by internalizing it. If we hate/love less the light, because of what we are doing, then it could stand to reason, that we hate/love less ourselves for what we are doing. In essence, the word hate could come to mean that we don't love ourselves enough because of the things that we may find ourselves doing that we know is not right.

Let me drive this point home to you. What is that one thing (or more) that you are doing that you hate about yourself right now? I'm not talking about trivial matters. I am talking about things that you know are wrong. Things like; drinking too much, using illegal drugs, pornography, etc.

These are things you do where no one can see you doing them (the darkness). You may be at the point where you don't want anyone to see or know what you are doing. In other words, you don't want this secret to come to light. Why is that? Could it be that you secretly hate yourself every time you give in to these desires? That is why we cover these things up with excuses and hide them in the dark.

If you have come this far into this book then you are serious about getting your life back on track. If you really are ready to eradicate the self-sabotage in your life then you need to start by eliminating the excuses. Excuses are meant for one thing only, to cover things up. In order for you to be truly free you have to allow the light to shine on your life. This is the only way to get rid of the darkness. Darkness cannot peacefully coexist with light. Light always wins over the darkness.

If you want to be in the light then you have to make sure you surround yourself with people who have the light in them. In 1 Corinthians 15:33, the Apostle Paul writes; *"Do not be deceived; 'Bad company corrupts good morals.'"* You may not be strong enough to shine the light on yourself, but when you surround yourself with good accountability, you don't have to. They will do it for you.

If you are serious about your freedom and desire to eliminate this type of hate in your life then you must surround yourself with strong accountability. You can't do it alone, so don't even try it. Allow God to work in your life through others. That is mostly the way He works anyways.

As we conclude this section I want you to do one thing for me. I want you to think of one or more people that you could surround yourself with. People, that will call you out when you start to drift back into the darkness. And if there is one person that first came to your mind but then you dismissed them because you thought they would be too hard on you.

That is the one I want you to choose. That is someone who will be brutally honest with you and help to keep you walking in the light and not the darkness. Someone who will walk with you and hopefully help teach you to eliminate the hate from your life.

Neutralize Your Entitlement

The "E" in *H.E.L.L.* stands for **E**ntitlement. If hate is in essence, not loving yourself enough. Then entitlement, is the opposite, loving yourself too much. Let's look at the definition of entitlement. Since "entitlement" is simply the state of being entitled, let's look at that definition. Entitled simply means; "to give (a person or thing) a title, right, or claim to something; furnish with grounds for laying a claim"[3]

So from this we can conclude that entitlement is the state of a person feeling they have a right or claim to something. It is an approach to life in general that says everything is or should be mine. It is an attitude that tends to focus inwardly upon you and not caring about others around you. Its end goal is to satisfy your innermost ambitions, desires, and greed.

Let's look at Mark 7:20-23, NKJV; "*...it is what comes from within that defiles you. From within, out of a person's heart, come evil thoughts, sexual immorality, theft, murder, adultery, greed, wickedness, deceit, lustful desires, envy, slander, pride, and foolishness. All these things come from within; they are what defile you.*"

When I read those verses, a stark reality hits me. It's almost as if the writer is talking about today's society. Entitlement has become the norm in our culture. It seems that everything today is about my rights, my claims, or my title. We seem to have forgotten the words of Jesus to "*Do to others whatever you would like them do to you...*" (Matthew 7:12 NLT)

This is especially true in the life of an addict or someone that is fully captured in the bondage of life-controlling problems. Everything is centered on themselves. It is an attitude that says, it's all about me and I don't care what happens to everyone else.

Maybe you can relate to this type of an attitude. Maybe, just maybe, if you are totally honest with yourself, you will even admit to that kind of an attitude. It's ok for now. The first step toward getting better is to identify where you are. Once you know what you are struggling with, you can begin your road to healing.

Entitlement is an ugly little monster in the beginning. But like every "little" monster, it has a big appetite. It is this appetite that causes it to grow into a big monster that devours everything in its path. If you can capture this monster before it grows too big, then your recovery is shorter. Sadly, most people not only let it grow, but they also feed it multiple times daily. The end result is a personal disaster of biblical proportions.

When entitlement is strongly entrenched in your life, it consumes every fiber of your being. You can't see that the problems you are having are because of you. You falsely believe that everyone is out to get you and take everything away from you that you love and hold dear.

Entitlement is also the reason a lot of people self-sabotage. They feel they have "earned" something because of their success in sobriety. There have even been people that I have known that would go out and celebrate the graduation from a recovery program by getting "wasted." When confronted with the reality of what they had done, their response was that they; "had earned it."

So what is the secret to overcoming entitlement? It is simple humility. You need to continually be in servant mode. You need to always be looking for the next opportunity to serve someone or some cause that is bigger than you.

What is your passion? What is it that gets your juices flowing whenever you think about doing this? That is where you need to look to find occasions to serve. You were created for success and part of finding that success is helping other people find their success. If we are too busy helping other people succeed then we are too busy to feel sorry for ourselves. If we stop feeling sorry for ourselves then we will stop feeling as if the world owes us. If the truth of the matter is told, we are the ones who owe more than anyone could ever owe to us.

Neutralize Your Lack

In Hosea 4:6 NKJV we can read the following; "*My people are destroyed for a **lack** of knowledge...*" The dictionary defines lack, when used as a noun to be; "*a deficiency or absence of something needed, desirable, or customary.*"[4] However, when we look at the original language of Hebrew that the Old Testament was written in it comes from a word that means, "*to be nothing or not exist.*"[5] It is also important to understand what this scripture is referring to as having a lack of. In this case it is a lack of knowledge, and the way that knowledge is used here is significant. In the original Hebrew language it means, *"to know by seeing, observation, care, recognition."*[6]

When we put these two words together using the original language the truth begins to manifest itself. Basically what Hosea was trying to tell the people of his day was this. They are being destroyed by not having an observation of the truth of God in their life. Let me say that this is where you may also find yourself in the day and age that we live in.

Self-sabotage tends to occur in our life because we no longer have first hand observation of what the truth is supposed to look like to us. For some of you, you may have never really known the truth God was trying to speak into your life. For others, somewhere along your journey, you lost sight of that truth as you found yourself spiraling deeper and deeper down a dark hole with no visible form of escape.

If you find yourself here, it is important to understand that there is hope. There is always hope as long as there is still breath in your body. The all-loving, all-powerful, God of the universe wants to show you how to get your life back on the right path and keep it there. It is possible, and it is not as hard as you may think it is.

First, you have to identify that you do have Lack, or in our definition, a deficiency of seeing God's truth in your life. But in truth, this is not really the case. Let me prove it to you. If you will just reflect on your life for a few minutes you will begin to see that there have been a few times when things happened to you that simply could not be explained. Things such as; an unexpected gift from someone you hadn't heard from in a while, a phone call from that friend you thought you had burned your bridges with, or even a call from a loved one just to tell you how much you were loved. And even if none of those things have happened to you yet, you are here right now reading this book and learning about it. A book that you thought you would never read in a million years. Yet, here you are, hanging on to the words as if your life depended on it.

What does all this mean? That brings me to my second point. This means that somewhere, somehow, there is a power, higher than you at work in your life. He is looking out for you and trying to show you the truth of whom you are, and were created to be. I personally like to call this Higher Power; God. You can dismiss things like this all day long as coincidences. However, I have learned that in the midst of coincidences, there is usually an underlying theme tying things together.

I know, you are getting impatient and want to know how all of this works together to help you overcome self-sabotage. Check this out, first you find out you're missing something in your life. Then you find out that someone or something as been working behind the scenes to show you what it is that you're missing. Now we get to my third and final point on this subject. God creates boundaries in your life to get you and keep you on the right path.

Look at this scripture; *"Jesus said to the people who believed in him, 'You are truly my disciples if you remain faithful to my teachings. And you will know the truth, and the truth will set you free.'"* (John 8:31-32, NLT). His teachings are the Word of God (The Bible). The Bible is a set of instructions that are designed to help us navigate life here on earth. In other words, it is directions on building boundaries in your life to help keep you safe from things that would destroy you for your "lack" of not knowing the truth.

I know, I know. No one likes to talk about boundaries. It is restrictive and it sometimes keeps us from doing what we want to do. But boundaries are also put into place to protect us from things on the other side of the fence. If you want to be successful in life, you have to create boundaries for yourself that you know are dangerous to your success.

Not only do you need these boundaries in your life, you need to tell other people you trust about them. This is why accountability is such an important aspect of your success in recovery. If no one around you knows what those boundaries are, then they can't help you stay within them. Having boundaries in your life are the key to protecting your truth and kicking the H.E.L.L. of "lack" out of your life.

Neutralize Your Lust

Well here we are. For some of you, I know you have been anxiously waiting for this moment in the book. You want to know what I am going to say about Lust. Before we start let's look at what John had to say in 1 John 2:16-17 NKJV; *"For all that is in the world—the **lust** of the flesh, the lust of the eyes, the pride of life—is not of the Father but is of the world. And the world is passing away, and the lust of it; but he who does the will of God abides forever."*

I can make an educated guess that some of you are wanting to know just how in the world can you kick lust out of your life. It is such a part of the world that we live in it seems impossible to do. In order to understand how to get rid of it we must first understand what it is. So let's look at the definitions.

The dictionary defines lust as, *"an intense sexual desire or appetite."*[7] In fact, in our society at large, lust has become known to be synonymous for sexual desire. It is not unusual to hear someone talking about this whenever they see someone they desire to make a remark like; "I think I'm in lust." But let's take a look at the original language it was written in. It means a; *"desire, craving, longing, desire for what is forbidden."*[8] Here is more generic in nature and simply means a desire. The actual usage here has an emphasis on that which is forbidden.

The same word is used in James 4:5 KJV; *"Do ye think that the scripture saith in vain, The spirit that dwelleth in us lusteth to envy?"* This is the same root word that is being used in this verse. However, in this case it is a variation of the word that means a strong desire for what is good. Or in other words, the Holy Spirit has a strong desire, craving or longing to give us more grace in order to do God's will.

The word lust as used by John is in stark contrast to this as he is basically painting a picture of someone who is determined to do the wrong things because of having a wrongful desire. This is what gets a lot of people in trouble. It also leads a lot of individuals to make poor decision that will inevitably lead to self-sabotage.

Self-sabotage takes place in a person's life because they are not satisfied with where they are in life. Because of this a strong desire begins to form in them until it reaches the point of no return. It is then acted upon and the end result is usually some consequence that will stay with a person far longer than the actual deed may have taken.

God did not intend for us to act like animals that have no control over their basic instincts. He created us in His image and charged us with taking care of His creation. In that, we have failed miserably on all fronts. However, God sent us His son; Jesus, to get us back on the right path again.

Self-control is not just a concept that you read about in the Bible or other books. It is a way of life. It is making a statement that I choose to not get kicked around by my desires that are out of control. God created me with a spirit in His image. And the spirit that He placed within me will bear fruit is it is tended to, and one of those fruits in called; self-control. I know, I lost some of you right there. I can hear you whining; "You don't know where I came from. How can I have self-control?" Spare me the words and thoughts because that is simply not true.

We all have some measure of self-control. If we did not, this world, as well as your personal world, would be full of chaos. For instance, you have self-control when you decide to make something to eat. You will wait patiently for it to cook or however it may be prepared before you eat it. If you did not, you would just eat it straight out of the package it came in. Another way you have self-control is waiting for people to return your phone calls. If you did not, you would be calling them back every fifteen seconds.

My point is that every day, every one exercises self-control in their life; people waiting in line at Starbucks®, cars waiting for a traffic light to turn, or waiting for Burger King® to give it to you your way. The thing that most people forget is that self-control is like a muscle. It will only get stronger if you exercise it. When you say no to a strong desire or lust, to do something forbidden, your self-control gets stronger. This in turn, allows you more strength to say no to a stronger desire next time.

What ever it is that you are struggling with, I want you to try a little experiment with me. The next time you give in to your desire, set a timer to see how long it is before the next time you have a desire to do it again. Then I want you to add five minutes to that time. For example; if you want to quit smoking cigarettes, time how long it takes after you smoke one until you have a desire to smoke another one. Then when the desire kicks in again add five minutes to your last time. The next time the desire hits, I want you to add five more minutes or ten minutes total to the last time. Keep adding five minutes every time until you have doubled your original time.

That my friend is how you exercise self-control and before you know it you have cut your smoking down to half of what it was before you started this experiment. It is not hard to do but it does take work on your part. It will not happen overnight. It will take time. However, little by little, you will begin to see improvement in whatever area of your life you apply this model to. You will have discovered that it is possible to kick the H.E.L.L. of Lust out of your life.

Do you have a strong enough desire to do it? If you have trouble trusting yourself to do this, then enlist the help of a good friend who will help you. Maybe you can even help them overcome something in their life that they have been struggling with. After all just like the scripture says in Ecclesiastes 4:9-10 NKJV; "*Two are better than one because they have good reward for their labor. For if they fall, one will lift up his companion. But woe to him who is alone when he falls, for he has no one to lift him up.*"

Conclusion

If you haven't guessed it by now then you probably never will. I love using acronyms to drive home a point. It is easy to remember and sometimes comical in the process. Take the four subsections above. The first word of each section is a letter in the word; H.E.L.L.

I believe excuses are straight from the pit of hell and you need to get them out of your life. I guess that is really what this chapter is all about. If you want to negate the forces of hell in your life then you need to kick the H.E.L.L. out of yourself and your vocabulary.

I already know. Some of the super-spiritual people are cringing in their shoes right now thinking I used the "H" word. Well, I did, and I didn't. You see, I used an acronym, so in my book, I'm not really cussing because it stands for something else. Anyway, that's my story and I'm sticking with it.

If you are ready to change your thinking and move on to another level of success then I dare you to continue. There is only one chapter left. You can do it. After all, you have come this far so why not finish what you started. Before continuing to the next chapter please do the exercises at the end of the chapter.

FOOTNOTES

[1] Santana, Carlos (n.d.). Excuses. Retrieved 11/6/2014 from http://www.brainyquote.com/quotes/keywords/excuses.html

[2] Webb, Brian T. Strong's KJV App (version 4.1.4), G3404, © 2008-2013.

[3] http://dictionary.reference.com/browse/entitle. Accessed on 12/11/14.

[4] http://dictionary.reference.com/browse/lack?s=t. Accessed on 1/24/15

[5] http://www.biblestudytools.com/lexicons/hebrew/nas/ayin.html. Accessed on 1/24/15

[6] http://www.biblestudytools.com/lexicons/hebrew/nas/daath.html. Accessed 1/24/15

[7] http://dictionary.reference.com/browse/lust?s=t. Accesses 1/24/15

[8] http://www.biblestudytools.com/lexicons/greek/nas/epithumia.html. Accessed 1/24/15

M.A.P. Your SOULUTION

Make a Plan
- Write down on a separate piece of paper, the one excuse you struggle with that leads you to self-sabotage your success.
- Now take some time to reflect back to the time you first used this excuse (You may need to ask friends or family to figure this out). Once you have figured that out write down the reasons you first started using this excuse.
- Now write out a counter point for every reason you wrote down.

Accept Accountability {Recruit Partner(s) to Keep You Focused}
- Go to your accountability partner and share with them everything you just wrote above.
- Ask them to call you out every time you use this excuse. The goal here is to eliminate this excuse from your life.

Put it into Action
- Make this exercise a regular part of your self-inventory process.
- Once you have kicked the excuse you listed above out of your, choose another one and use the same process until you have also kicked it out of your life.
- Repeat the process as often as needed.

NOTES

NOTES

S.H.A.R.E.

The Audacity of Grace

> *"The audacity of grace is the hardest thing, as a Christian, to deal with.*
> *We serve a God who pardons sins with no recollection.*
> *But, we live with minds that remember them, full well.*
> *Why can't we be like God? Why can't we forget, too?"*
> — *Serena Woods*[1]

John was involved in human trafficking. He was for all purposes, a slave trader. He had been the one responsible for herding and transporting people as if they were cattle. He would put them in such tight places that they would not be able to fully extend their legs or arms during long journeys in captivity. He knew what it was like to arrive at a new destination only to find that some of his cargo had died during their passage due to the poor care he had provided for them.

In spite of his hardness, there was a deep, hidden part of John that lived with the shame and memories of all the terrible events he had participated in as a human trafficker. He had done horrible and unspeakable things, simply because the money was so outrageous. John was good at what he did and made a decent living since he wasn't one to let his emotions step in the way of his performance. After all, it was just business.

John wasn't always like this. A noble Christian mother had raised him. In fact, she had hoped for her son to become a minister one day. She would teach him the scriptures at an early age. But she had died when he was still a child. He was only seven years old at the time of her death. His father was a sailor that soon remarried. His new mother was more into spending time with her friends than raising a son that wasn't really hers. So John was left to run the streets and hang out with other children that were the outcasts of their neighborhood. This led to him getting into all kinds of trouble on a regular basis.

Eventually, John followed in the footsteps of his father and grew up to be a sailor as well. That was where he had learned about the lucrative business of human trafficking. He eventually got out of the Navy to pursue a career in this well-paid enterprise. It wasn't long before he became heavily involved in it and began to slowly work his way up the ranks.

Then one night as John was transporting his "cargo" something happened to him. He had been thinking about his mother and all the beliefs she had taught him as a young child. He wondered if God truly did love him for all the wicked deeds he had done. He felt as if there was no way that God would ever forgive him for all the sins and evils he had committed. Suddenly, he found himself in the midst of a life-threatening storm and feared for his safety. In a moment of desperation he cried out for God to save him. God not only saved him but also delivered from all harm.

After this incident John turned his life around. He didn't immediately leave the business he was in. But he lost interest in it as he began to have feelings for the people he had helped enslave. Even though he treated them better than anyone else he couldn't keep doing this and trying to live a godly life. He eventually left and came to be involved in a church. This led to him finally being called into the ministry. He made the decision to go to seminary and soon became a pastor. He was even responsible for pastoring two churches at the same time.

I wish I could say that John was a graduate of our program. But the truth of the matter is that John is none other than John Newton. He is the man that wrote that sacred, old hymn; "Amazing Grace." He lived during the eighteenth century in England. My intent for this book was to only use stories of people that I had personally witnessed a true transformation take place in their life. But in writing this book with a chapter about the audacity of grace, I felt as if this was the most appropriate story to share.

What other person in history could I use to share the immense audacity of a grace so excessive that it could turn around even the greatest cynical sinner? And, if this audacious grace could turn a slave trader, like John Newton around, think of what that kind of grace can do for you. His life was impacted by grace in such a way that he made a lasting impact upon this world. Even though he has been dead for over two hundred years, people still talk about him and we still sing the hymn; "Amazing Grace." It was a hymn, which he wrote, 235 years ago.

So what is the audacity of grace? Audacity is defined as; *"boldness or daring, especially with confident or arrogant disregard for personal safety, conventional thought, or other restrictions; shameless boldness."*[2] While grace is defined as; *"a manifestation of favor, especially by a superior; mercy, clemency, pardon."*[3] When you put the two together you have quite the power phrase. I like to define it as: *A bold confidence of supernatural favor in a person's life that goes against conventional thoughts or restrictions.* That is the kind of audacious grace that John Newton had when he wrote "Amazing Grace" and is the same thing you will need to move past whatever is controlling your life into victory. But the great thing about this is that it is not just for you. It is for everyone. And part of your healing process is to S.H.A.R.E. it with everyone you come in contact with.

S.H.A.R.E. Your Significance

The implication of this type of grace is huge! Can you imagine how you would live your life if you did this? Living your life with a bold confidence would be life changing for you. You would walk around believing that your life was significant. Not because of anything you had done. It would only be by the grace of an all-knowing, all-powerful God.

All of this is from a God who wants to be so intimately involved in every detail of your life. And He wants to do all this, in spite of everything that you have done or ever would do. The infinite God of the universe has showered this kind of audacious grace on your life. So the question is; "What are you going to do about it?"

The reason I ask you that question is because the other side of this message is that you can't keep this type of grace to yourself. It is too big. The message is meant to influence more people than just you. You were meant to share this significance so that others can realize the importance of this life-altering truth. The impact of this idea is profound; you are important to God. He loves you more than you could ever imagine.

In fact, He has gone to great lengths to make sure you received this message. Think of all things that had to come into play at the exact moment, just to make sure you received this message of hope at the exact time you did. If it had been too early, you would not have listened. If it had been too late, you would have already moved on to something else. But at the exact moment that you needed it the most, He sent this message of hope to you. He sent this message at a time in your life where it would make the most sense to you. He sent this message of hope, from someone that was listening to God, to give you hope, when you needed it the most.

The reality of it all is this; God influenced someone to share this "audacious grace" with you and it was no accident. You are significant to Him. He cares about everything that you care about. He feels the pain of rejection and loneliness just like you do. You matter immensely to Him and He has gone to great lengths to make sure you know how much He cares for you.

He asks nothing in return for this overwhelming graciousness. However, He does encourage you to share your newly found significance with others just like you. An addicted lifestyle is seeped in selfishness. God wants you to break out of this lifestyle permanently by sharing this good news with others who need it the most. What God has done for you, He wants to do for everyone.

The best way to start this is to get involved in a local church by helping them serve other people. That is the secret to getting out of selfishness. It is ironic that we sometimes will spend our entire life trying to be somebody significant and fail miserably. But when we make a conscious decision to turn everything over to God, and serve others in the process, God makes us more significant than we ever imagined possible.

Think about this for a moment. I want you to close your eyes and think of the worst possible thing that you have ever done in your life. Think of that moment as a picture in a frame. Now I want you to imagine you are there on the hill the day that Jesus is being crucified. You are walking up to him hanging there on the cross. You see him hanging there in humiliation gasping for breath and blood running down the cross.

As you stand there you have this overwhelming sense of shame, like you had something to do with this. You kneel at the cross and the tears begin to flow uncontrollably. You place the picture of that awful moment at the foot of the cross and you bury your head in your hands. Then, in the midst of your sorrow you feel something. You feel different. You look up and as you start to look around you notice that the picture you laid at the foot of the cross is covered in Jesus' blood. You can't even make out the picture at all. It is completely covered in blood and you can't see what it is about anymore.

That, my friend, is audacious grace. That is why you are significant. Not because of anything you have done. You are significant because of the price the Jesus paid for you to be free from the worst sin you could ever imagine. Not just that sin, but every sin you have ever committed. You are significant, you are loved, and you have value and worth because someone paid for you and he placed value, worth, love, and significance on you before you were ever born. How can you not share that type of significance?

S.H.A.R.E. Your Hope

The audacity of grace will also cause you to have audacious hope. We have already talked about hope in a previous chapter. While hope, in itself, is it's own soulution, the kind of hope we are talking about here goes beyond just finding hope for you. It is a belief in yourself, that you are able to make a difference in this world.

This is not because of anything you have done or accomplished. It is not the result of any achievements that you have been blessed to accomplish in life. It is quite simply the end result of placing your life in God's hands and letting Him make a difference through you.

In fact, this kind of hope is a new kind of hope that goes beyond any type of expectation you have ever felt before. It is an anticipation of knowing, that by you sharing your story of redemption, others have come to a safe place of healing in their hearts as well. The very place of your own personal pain has now become a launching pad for the passion your newfound determination in life.

You have now moved into a different state of living. It is a realm that helps others overcome the pain of their own past. But it goes beyond just simple hope. It is a hope that things are so different now that you have the strength to finally face the fears. Fears, that have paralyzed you, for far too long.

And, by finally overcoming those fears, you now have a purpose in life. You can finally understand the big picture. Life is not just about you anymore. It is no longer about what you can get out of this life. There has been a major shift in your thinking. You now ponder how you can help other people find their own purpose in life.

There is such a freedom in this type of thinking. You are no longer thinking selfishly. For once in your life, you find that other people matter just as much, if not more than you. You actually look forward to talking to people and sharing what God has done for you. After all, who knows more than you what you were going through? Yet instead of living your life in all the hurts of the past, you are now walking in healing, toward the future. A future, that for maybe the first time in your life, looks bright and full of hope.

And, it is this hope that continues to make a difference in your life. It is this hope that gives you energy to wake up every day. It is this hope that allows you the freedom to move forward and face any adversity that life my throw your way. It is this hope that, at the end of the day, allows you to close your eyes in sleep and know that everything is all right. Don't forget to S.H.A.R.E. your hope with others who are lacking. You may be the only hope out of the chaos they are in. It is like they are standing on a street in the path of a speeding car. They are frozen with fear and can't move. It is up to you to push them out of the way of certain danger.

That is the hope you have. That is the hope you must S.H.A.R.E. You can't keep it to yourself. It is way too valuable for any one person to hoard it all.

Think back to when you were in your mess. How many people did you coerce into joining your chaotic lifestyle? Now you have the opportunity to S.H.A.R.E. the hope that transformed your life into something amazing...something audacious. Don't keep that hope within you. Let everyone you know see what hope has done in your life.

S.H.A.R.E. Your Authenticity

In the process of sharing your hope, it becomes evident that you must possess a genuine faith is something higher than yourself. Without this genuineness, it doesn't mean anything. People can see right through fake. Actually, they can spot it a mile or more away. It stands out like a sore thumb. Hope, by its own very nature, is meant to establish a legitimate atmosphere of faithfulness.

You can't have hope without faith, and you can't have faith without hope. The two go hand in hand. When you are in a position to share with others, it is important to remember where you came from. You need to have a sincere and honest approach of how you came to experience this hope. The way to do this is to be completely authentic. There is no other way.

No doubt you can remember back to a time when you were in your own mess. You knew how to read people and then work them to your advantage. Nothing much has changed since then. People who are struggling with life-controlling issues are continually looking for ways to validate their choices. One way they do this is to find fault in those trying to help them out of their mess. If they can discredit their rescuer, they can continue to justify their actions.

That is what being authentic is so important. When you are being absolutely genuine, there is a certain dependability that goes hand in hand with that. If you are "for real" then people know they can depend upon you to be "real" with them.

This is especially true when you are dealing with people who are stuck in their circumstances. They need someone reliable to help them out of their hole. You have the answers to their problem. They need to know that no matter what they may have done, there is a loving Savior who is willing and able to shower them with His audacious grace. So, let your grace shine with an authentic passion that makes a difference to all you come in contact with.

S.H.A.R.E. Your Reason Why

In the process of being significant, hopeful, and authentic, you must never forget the reason why you got out of your mess. This is the cause you must fight for on a daily basis. It is the motivation that fuels your transformation.

As humans, we tend to be goal oriented. Whether that is for finding food, shelter, or companionship. This orientation is what drives us to succeed. If we want to be successful and help others be successful, then we must continually have a purpose that is the 'wind beneath our wings."

No matter what status in life you came from, you were motivated from a very young age to continually be moving toward a goal. Whether it was talking, walking, finishing school, or finding a spouse. Everything in life is usually motivated by something.

There is nothing wrong with being motivated to do something. It is the reasoning behind your motivation that makes it either good or bad. Which do you choose? Which do you want to help people around you choose? That, my friend, is your reason why!

Whatever thoughts may come into play as you read this section is what will determine your outlook on this concept. What do you want to accomplish with your life? Do you want to just barely squeak by, or do you want to fling the doors open wide as you walk in?

S.H.A.R.E. Your Experience

So far we have talked about sharing; your significance, your hope, your authenticity, and your reason why. As we wrap things up I want to close by talking about the importance of sharing your experience. I know that some of you might wonder about that. You might be thinking; "What is so special about my experiences worth sharing? I would just as soon forget them."

I will agree with you that sometimes it is best to forget some experiences. However, I have discovered that most of who I am today comes from the sum total of my life experiences, the good and the bad. The secret is in knowing when to share the appropriate experience at just the right time where it will have the most impact. And as the old English proverb says; "Practice make perfect."

There is a quote that states; "Knowledge is power"[4]. Therefore, if this is true, it would be reasonable to assume that the more knowledge you could obtain, the more powerful you could become in that particular area. Of course, the areas we are talking about here are being and maintain your freedom over the life-controlling problems in your life. The more you know about overcoming setbacks, hurts, and inner turmoil, the better your understanding of the experiences you need will become clear.

Let's face it, the better your experience at something is, the more likely you will be successful at it. If you have come this far in the process, then you are somewhat successful. And, in the process, you have developed skills that will not only help you, but others as well. That is why you must share these experiences. What has helped you, could help someone else dealing with the same circumstances.

It also should go without saying that if you have reached a level of success, it is then your duty share that knowledge with others who may be dealing with the same inner chaos as yourself. This is especially true if you find yourself encountering someone who fits this description. I don't believe in coincidences, and neither should you. God gives us divine encounters for a reason. And they usually involve some healing for others as well as our self. And this brings us back to the beginning of this chapter.

The suffering that Jesus endured on the cross was so that we could partake in this audacious grace. It is what creates transformation. We cannot be transformed on our own. It takes the audacity of a grace so overwhelming that it is impossible to resist. You come to a crossroad and know that if you don't choose the right path, then it is over. So you become desperate and cry out for help to make the right decision. It is then your privilege to show others how this kind of grace works.

You have the power, because you have the experience that gave you the knowledge. Share your experiences with others who are struggling. You will find that in the end it will help you more than it helps them.

FOOTNOTES

[1] http://www.graceisforsinners.com/the-audacity-of-grace/#ixzz320dbpxLl Under Creative Commons License: Attribution Non-Commercial No Derivatives

[2] audacity. (n.d.). Dictionary.com Unabridged. Retrieved October 27, 2014, from Dictionary.com website: http://dictionary.reference.com/browse/audacity

[3] grace. (n.d.). Dictionary.com Unabridged. Retrieved October 27, 2014, from Dictionary.com website: http://dictionary.reference.com/browse/grace

[4] Sir Francis Bacon, *Religious Meditations, Of Heresies, 1597 English author, courtier, & philosopher (1561 – 1626)*

M.A.P. Your SOULUTION

Make a Plan
- On a separate piece of paper write your testimony out. You should aim for no more than 2-5 minutes.
- Use the following formula to help you come up with your story;
  - o **A**ctivating Event – What is the one thing that happened to you that led you to a downward spiral. This is usually some form of trauma (physical, emotional, spiritual) that has contributed to your life-controlling problems.
  - o **B**ehaviors – What are the behaviors that are a direct result of the trauma in your life from your activating event? These are your attempts to deaden your pain.
  - o **C**onsequences – What are the consequences that are a direct result of your behaviors?
  - o **D**reams – What are your dreams? Include your lost dreams you had as well as new ones.
  - o **E**xpectations – What are your expectations moving forward.
  - o **F**inish – Wrap it up and finish strong.
  - o **G**ive Thanks – Appreciate the people who have helped you. Avoid Oscar speeches.

Accept Accountability {Recruit Partner(s) to Keep You Focused}
- Once you have your story written out share it with someone you trust.
- Ask for constructive criticism.

Put it into Action
- Look for opportunities to share your story.
- This could be AA or CR meetings or people you meet that are struggling the same way you used to.

NOTES

NOTES

BIBLIOGRAPHY

Amen, D. (2005). *Making a Good Brain Great.* New York, NY: Three Rivers Press.

The American Heritage® Dictionary of the English Language, (4th ed.). (2004). Houghton Mifflin Company

Anderson, N. & Quarles, M. (2003). *Over oming Addictive Behavior.* Ventura, CA: Regal Books.

Anderson, N. (2000). *Victory Over the Darkness.* Ventura, CA: Regal Books.

Barnett, M. (2011). *The Cause Within You.* Carol Stream, IL: Tyndale House Pubishers.

Bartholomew, N., Dansereau, D., and Simpson, D., Editors. (2006). *Getting Motivated to Change.* Fort Worth, TX. TCU Institute of Behavioral Research.

Bassett, L. (2011). *The Solution: Conquer Your Fear, Control Your Future.* New York, NY: Sterling Publishing Co. Inc.

Covey, S. (1994). *First Things First.* New York, NY: Simon Schuster Inc.

Covey, S. (1989). *The 7 Habits of Highly Effective People.* New York, NY: Simon & Schuster Inc.

Dye, M. (2006). *The Genesis Process for Change Groups, Book 2, Individual Workbook.* Self-published.

Elliot, E. (1989). *In the Shadow of the Almighty.* New York, NY: HarperCollins Publishers.

Elliot, E. (1981). *Through the Gates of Splendor.* Carol Stream, IL: Tyndale House Publishers.

Gehring, T. (2012). *Settle It! ...and be Blessed.* Orlando, FL: Montserrat.

Hersh, S. (2008). *The Last Addiction.* Colorado Springs, CO: WaterBrook Press.

Luck, K. (2006). *Risk: Are You Willing to Trust God with Everything?* Colorado Springs, CO: WaterBrook Press.

Mason, J. (2012). *Let Go of Whatever Holds You Back.* Grand Rapids, MI: Revell.

May, G. (1988). *Addiction and Grace: Love and Spirituality in the Healing of Additions.* New York, NY: HarperCollins Publishers.

May, G. (2004). *The Dark Night of the Soul.* New York, NY: HarperCollins Publishers.

Meyer, J. (2005). *Approval Addiction: Overcoming Your Need to Please Everyone.* New York, NY: Time Warner Book Group

Perkins, B. (2000). *Awaken the Leader Within.* Grand Rapids, MI: Zondervan.

Prentiss, C. (2006). *The Alcoholism Cure.* Los Angeles, CA: Power Press.

Stone, J. (1989). *Frustrated Grace.* Cleveland, TN: White Wing Publishing House and Press.

Stone, J. (1990). *The Grace of God: A Handbook for Christian Growth.* Cleveland, TN: White Wing Publishing House and Press.

Urschel, H. (2009). *Healing the Addicted Brain.* Naperville, IL: SourceBooks Inc.

Wilson, H. (2008). *Put Your Addiction in Remission: The Secret for Sobriety.* Retrieved August 9, 2009 from http://www.addictioninremission.com.

ABOUT THE AUTHOR

Michael Conner is currently serving as the Executive Director of the DC Discipleship Recovery Program at Theπ Dream Center in Los Angeles, CA. He serves under the leadership of Pastors; Tommy & Matthew Barnett. While in this position he has been responsible for the recovery of thousands of individuals. Part of his responsibilities has included overseeing up to two hundred people on a daily basis.

His work in the recovery ministry started back in 1999 when he took a job at the City Rescue Mission in Oklahoma City, OK. Nothing could have prepared him for the passion and fulfillment he has experienced ever since that June day. Even though that was the start of his professional recovery career, it wasn't until 2007 that he and his wife; Vilma became certified addictions counselors.

Michael is currently a Master's Level – Registered Addiction Specialist in the state of California. He also has an Associates degree in Practical Ministries as well as a Bachelor's degree in Addiction Studies with a Biblical emphasis. He has been a licensed minister since 1980 and has held various positions in ministry; Youth Pastor, Singles Pastor, Associate Pastor, and Sr. Pastor.

He was born in Tulsa, Oklahoma and has been married to his wife Vilma since 2004. He has a grown daughter, two grandsons, and two dogs.

Michael is an established speaker, teacher, mentor, coach, and author. If you are interested in contacting him for speaking engagements you may reach him by email at the following address; miraconenterprises@gmail.com or by phone at 669-247-SOUL (7685).

Printed in Australia
AUOC02n1002231015
271192AU00010B/13/P